SCIENCE AND STATE GOVERNMENT

PUBLISHED FOR

THE INSTITUTE FOR RESEARCH IN SOCIAL SCIENCE

BY

THE UNIVERSITY OF NORTH CAROLINA PRESS

SCIENCE AND STATE GOVERNMENT

*A Study of the Scientific Activities of
State Government Agencies in Six States*

BY

FREDERIC N. CLEAVELAND

THE UNIVERSITY OF NORTH CAROLINA PRESS
CHAPEL HILL

Foreword

THE SCIENTIFIC ACTIVITIES of the United States federal government have been treated in a number of significant studies in recent years, yet virtually no attempt has been made to explore the role of state governments in the scientific effort of the nation. In March, 1954, the National Science Foundation, recognizing the need for developing systematic information about the scientific activities of state governments, entered into contract with the Institute for Research in Social Science at the University of North Carolina to undertake a study of the scientific programs in six states. The results of the investigations are presented here.

The immediate task of the study has been one of description: to report on the nature of the research and related scientific undertakings in which state government agencies are engaged; to measure these endeavors in terms of dollar expenditures and professional manpower investment; to discover the place of scientific activity in the various fields of state government operation; to identify the kinds of policies the states have formulated to guide their scientific activities; and to find out how these activities are organized and placed in the structure of state government administration. The larger task beyond inventory and description has been one of analysis and appraisal, requiring a look at research needs in comparison with existing research programs, an examination of state-federal relations in scientific activity, and an investigation of the work environment that state agencies provide for their scientists.

The states selected for examination are California, Connecticut, New Mexico, New York, North Carolina, and Wisconsin. Although no assumption was made that these six states are more representative of the forty-nine states than another six might be, an effort was made to insure a diversity in size, population, economic characteristics, political environment, and geographic location. A separate research team was established in each state under the direction of a resident state study director. The state study directors, the project director, and representatives of the National Science Foundation and the United States Bureau of the Census served as a central planning committee for the entire study. Members of the planning committee included the following:

California: Dr. Hubert R. Marshall, then Assistant Professor of Political Science, now Associate Professor, Stanford University.

Connecticut: Dr. Elroy P. Lehmann, then Assistant Professor of Geology, Wesleyan University, now engaged in paleontologic work as a geologist with Mobil Oil of Canada, Ltd. (Libyan Branch).

New Mexico: Dr. Allan R. Richards, Associate Professor of Government and Citizenship, University of New Mexico, now on leave serving in La Paz, Bolivia, as an advisor in personnel management at the School of Public Administration directed jointly by Universidad Mayor de San Andres and University of Tennessee in Bolivia.

New York: Dr. Clark D. Ahlberg, then Assistant Dean, College of Engineering, Syracuse University, now First Deputy Comptroller of the Division of the Budget, State of New York. Dr. Guthrie S. Birkhead, then Assistant Professor of Political Science, now Associate Professor and Chairman, Department of Political Science, Syracuse University.

North
Carolina: Dr. Frederic N. Cleaveland, then Assistant Professor of Political Science, now Professor and Chairman, Department of Political Science, University of North Carolina.

Wisconsin: Dr. Clara Penniman, then Assistant Professor of Political Science, now Associate Professor, University of Wisconsin.

National
Science
Foundation: Dr. John C. Honey, then Study Director for Government Research, National Science Foundation, now Executive Associate, The Carnegie Corporation.

                   Mr. Wayles Kennedy, Government Studies Staff.

                   Mrs. Mary S. Albert, Government Studies Staff.

Bureau of
the Census: Mr. Jacob M. Jaffe, Governments Division.

The detailed results of the studies have been recorded in six separate state reports prepared by the state study directors for the National Science Foundation;[1] these reports are yet to be published by the Institute for Research in Social Science, University of North Carolina, Chapel Hill. For this reason, references to the state reports can be given

[1]. The National Science Foundation has also issued its own report based upon this survey. See National Science Foundation, *Scientific Activities in Six State Governments, Summary Report on a Survey, Fiscal Year 1954* (Washington: Government Printing Office, 1958). This document presents in summary form a descriptive and factual account of the statistical findings of the survey of state government scientific activities.

only by chapter in the present work. The present report offers an interpretive comparison and summary of the findings in the six state reports. It bears some resemblance to the state reports in its organization and reflects much the same frame of reference. Although discussions in this summary are based on both descriptive and statistical details contained in the individual studies, these discussions are in no sense a duplication of the state reports. The emphasis on comparative analysis of the six states affords opportunity for insights and considerations different from those which concerned the state study directors in reporting on scientific activities in their particular states. The treatment here is directed towards achieving an overview of scientific research and related work as an activity of state government as such; accordingly, the richness of detail contained in the individual studies had to be sacrificed. Reference to specific agencies or particular research projects serves the purpose of illustration and cannot begin to cover the systematic description of these details in the separate state studies.

A brief preview of the seven chapters around which this study is organized may serve to give some insight into the concepts that guided the investigations.

The first chapter is devoted to a brief characterization of the six states. Scientific research, as any activity of state government, is carried on within a definable socio-economic, political, and cultural context. Each state study director discovered early in his work that he needed to know something of the nature of his state as a social entity and its political and governmental character. Without this background he could not comprehend the nature of the state's scientific effort. These background data provide the core of the initial chapter.

The second chapter presents the basic data for the comparative analysis of state scientific programs. The expenditures for scientific activities in fiscal year 1954 are examined and analyzed by area of governmental activity, character of research, and field of science. In addition, this chapter reviews the sources of funds used to finance the states' scientific work and compares the states' manpower investment in scientific activity.

Chapter III examines the distribution of scientific activity expenditures in each state among four major areas of governmental activity: agriculture; resource development and public works; health, education, and welfare; and higher education. The scientific programs within each area are discussed in terms of the emphasis given to them.

Chapter IV considers program administration of scientific activities, exploring policies guiding scientific programs; administrative organization for conducting research; planning and coordination of scientific work; and dissemination of the results of research and data collection. Chapter V is concerned with intergovernmental relations, seeking to describe how state and federal agencies work together in carrying out the states' scientific activities. Chapter VI devotes attention to state government as a place for research scientists to work.

The conclusion is a restatement of the major findings and implications of the study.

A note of caution must be entered concerning the statistical material. Much of the expenditure material presented in this study is based upon estimates rather than upon recorded figures. For the most part research is not set up in state budgets as an object of expenditure, and regular budget records often do not reveal actual amounts appropriated or spent for research projects. Although the study teams made every effort to obtain relevant and accurate information on costs and manpower, many of the figures are approximations arrived at with the help of informed state officials.

Furthermore, completely objective criteria have not always been available when classifying a state's scientific activities into the categories used in the study. Although members of the research staff spent hours in discussion, first among themselves and then with scores of agency officials in the six states, in an effort to develop a common understanding of these categories, some differences in interpretation have undoubtedly occurred. Happily, the most troublesome classification problems have arisen in the case of minor programs involving relatively small expenditures and limited manpower investment.

For all of us who have participated in this study in the six states, the effort has been a rewarding experience in many ways. We join in expressing sincere gratitude to the countless numbers of state officials who gave freely of their time and energies to answer our questions and supply the information we sought. We carry with us from these contacts a greater awareness of the dedication to public service and the continuing effort towards high professional attainment which generally characterize the scientific staffs of our state governments. This document and the six supporting studies are a report of their contribution to the nation.

> FREDERIC N. CLEAVELAND
> Project Director and
> Research Professor in the
> Institute for Research in
> Social Science,
> University of North Carolina

Chapel Hill, N. C.
June 15, 1959

Acknowledgments

IN A VERY REAL SENSE this study has been a group activity, dependent upon the willing cooperation of many people. The contribution of every member has been essential to its success.

I wish to express my sincere appreciation to the National Science Foundation for the financial support which made the project possible. More particularly, I want to acknowledge my indebtedness to the Foundation's Government Studies Staff, and especially to Mrs. Mary S. Albert and Mr. Wayles Kennedy for their keen interest and effective help at many stages in the study. Dr. Richard G. Axt and Dr. Donald N. Michael merit special commendation for their part in making available the data on the state universities. In addition, Dr. Jacob Perlman, Head of the Office of Special Studies, and Mrs. Mildred C. Allen and Mrs. Virginia B. Shapley of his staff have earned my gratitude for their invaluable assistance in bringing the entire project through to publication.

The central burden of research planning, conduct of field work, and preparation of the individual state reports fell upon the shoulders of the research staff recruited especially for this project. The value of the research product derives largely from their work. I am deeply grateful to each for his significant contribution and for his patient tolerance in surmounting the difficulties of a group research effort with the participants scattered over the country. My sincere thanks, then, to Dr. Clark Ahlberg and Dr. Guthrie S.

Birkhead in New York, Dr. Elroy Lehmann in Connecticut, Dr. Hubert Marshall in California, Dr. Clara Penniman in Wisconsin, and Dr. Allan Richards in New Mexico. Despite all the difficulties encountered in the project, our personal associations have made it a rewarding experience.

Turning to the local scene, I want to recognize the important contribution of Mr. Claude J. Johns, Jr., who was far more than a graduate research assistant, which title he bore for the eighteen months he devoted to the study. I also wish to pay special tribute to Mrs. Frances Schnibben and the secretarial staff of the Institute for Research in Social Science for their painstaking care in handling the reproduction of each manuscript.

Finally, I owe a special debt of gratitude to Dr. John C. Honey, formerly Study Director for Government Research in the National Science Foundation. He has seen the project through from start to finish and has shared many of the burdens but few of the satisfactions of project director. His contribution of stimulating ideas, searching criticism, and unfailing support and encouragement cannot be measured. Whatever merit the final research product has may be traced directly to his guidance and counsel.

Statements in this report are, of course, not the responsibility of the National Science Foundation. Errors of fact or interpretation are the full responsibility of the author.

Each of the six state reports contains its own acknowledgment of the splendid cooperation of countless state government officials. Their contribution was indeed central to the entire project. As project director, I should like to add my word of thanks to these devoted public servants.

Contents

Figures

Tables

SCIENCE AND STATE GOVERNMENT

I

The States

Don K. Price, Dean of the Littauer School of Public Administration, Harvard University, in the preface to *Government and Science*, discusses his convictions on the role of science in government which motivated him to write this book. He states:

> The deeper reason [for writing this book] was a notion that had been developing in my mind for several years . . . that the development of public policy and of the methods of its administration owed less in the long run to the processes of conflict among political parties and social or economic pressure groups than to the more objective processes of research and discussion among professional groups. . . . I was struck by the way in which a professional consensus, based on the findings of research of a scientific or semiscientific nature, often brought about the adoption of a new public policy and determined the method of its administration.[1]

This series of studies on the scientific activities of six state governments during 1954 is much more limited in objective than the testing of the proposition Dean Price advanced. Yet these studies, like the Price book, do seek to explore the relation of science and government. Furthermore, underlying the studies is the assumption that "the development of public policy and of the methods of its administration" at the state level is significantly affected by

1. D. K. Price, *Government and Science: Their Dynamic Relation in American Democracy* (New York: New York University Press, 1954), p. v.

this scientific work state agencies carry on and by the research skills acquired by public servants in the process. The individual state reports have presented a wealth of detail about research and development and related scientific activities in the agencies of the six states. These studies represent a first step towards discovering and analyzing the kind of role science plays in state government. This Summary Report, by looking back over the more detailed accounts in the state reports, attempts to develop tentative generalizations about the relation of science to state government. To do this requires consideration of the manner in which scientific programs have developed in the six states, the substance of these programs, the nature of policies governing scientific activity, the organizational forms and governmental relationships which have evolved in the conduct of scientific activities, and the working environment for scientists provided by the states.

THE SIX STATES: THEIR SOCIAL,

ECONOMIC, AND DEMOGRAPHIC CHARACTERISTICS[2]

In terms of the simple measures of socio-economic and demographic character, the six states afford a wide range of diversity. Ranking the states by area, for example, reveals that the sample includes the second and fourth largest states (California and New Mexico) and one of the smallest (Connecticut). The remaining three rank close to the middle

2. This discussion draws heavily upon information contained in the introductory chapters of the individual state reports which were prepared for the National Science Foundation as a part of this study and which are on file at the Institute for Research in Social Science, University of North Carolina: G. S. Birkhead and C. D. Ahlberg, Science and State Government in New York; F. N. Cleaveland and C. Johns, Science and State Government in North Carolina; E. P. Lehmann, Science and State Government in Connecticut; H. Marshall, Science and State Government in California; C. Penniman, Science and State Government in Wisconsin; A. R. Richards and G. Radosevich, Science and State Government in New Mexico (hereafter cited as New York Report, North Carolina Report, and so forth).

(Wisconsin twenty-fifth, North Carolina twenty-seventh, and New York twenty-ninth). In terms of population as of 1954, two of the most populous states are included; four states ranked in the top fifteen, and none ranked lower than thirty-eighth. Economic factors are equally diverse in the six states. For example, in terms of per capita income for the year 1953, California, Connecticut, and New York are above the national average (Connecticut and New York rank among the first four), Wisconsin is at the average, and New Mexico and North Carolina are well below. There are also certain characteristics that the six states have in common. The following discussion will draw particular attention to these, as well as to the unique features distinguishing a particular state from most or all of the others across the country.

Demographic Characteristics

Four of the states experienced moderate population growth in the 1940-50 decade, whereas the two western states grew at a very fast rate. Growth rates in New York, Wisconsin, North Carolina, and Connecticut ranged from 9.5 to 18 per cent; Connecticut was above the national average of 14.5 per cent, the other three somewhat below. California grew at the fantastic rate of 53.3 per cent, topping all forty-eight states; New Mexico placed eighth with a growth rate of 28 per cent.[3]

A substantial part of this growth in all forty-eight states occurred in urban and metropolitan areas. Connecticut, New York, and California ranked within the first seven in terms of degree of urbanization, reporting from 77 to 85 per cent of their people living in urban places in 1950 as compared to a national average of 64 per cent. Wisconsin, New Mexico, and North Carolina also urbanized rapidly, but the decennial census in 1950 reported that the percentage of their

3. United States Department of Commerce, *Statistical Abstract of the United States, 1955* (Washington: Government Printing Office, 1955), Table 12, p. 17.

population dwelling in urban areas was less than the national average.[4]

In contrast to the other five states—and indeed to the other forty-seven—North Carolina's population in 1950 was divided almost evenly among three classes: urban, rural farm, and rural non-farm (about 33 per cent each). Wisconsin, with a 58 per cent urban population, reported approximately the same proportion of her people (21 per cent) in the rural non-farm category as in the rural farm group. In the other four states the ratio of the rural non-farm to rural farm ranged from about 1½:1 to 6:1.[5] These ratios indicate that the urban character of these four states is more pronounced than the percentage of the people living in urban areas suggests. In all but North Carolina and Wisconsin more than half of the people living in rural areas do not earn their living through farming but rather are engaged in non-rural occupations. Many of these rural non-farm people are likely to be more urban than rural in their values and way of life.

Socio-economic Characteristics

Five of the six states (all but New Mexico) claim an important place among the manufacturing states of the country. In terms of the standard measure of value added by manufacturing, New York ranked first in the nation in 1953 with total value added of over $14.4 billion. California ranked sixth, Wisconsin tenth, Connecticut twelfth, and North Carolina fourteenth.[6] New York alone contains about one-fifth of all the manufacturing establishments in the nation and has built up an exceedingly diversified manufacturing economy. Between 1947 and 1953 both California and New Mexico doubled the annual figure for value added by manufacture. Even though New Mexico still ranks low among the states in value added (forty-fourth in 1953), the rate of

---

4. *Ibid.*, Table 19, pp. 26-27.   5. *Ibid.*
6. *Ibid.*, Table 1004, p. 817.

growth suggests the boom in New Mexico's current industrial development. Of special note in the other three states are Wisconsin's leadership in the machine tool and metal industries; Connecticut's progress in aircraft, electronics, and specialty manufacturing; and North Carolina's continued prominence in the manufacture of tobacco products, textiles, and forest products.

In the five states with significant manufacturing industry, factory payrolls accounted for 20 to 40 per cent of total income payments to individuals in 1953. Connecticut (40 per cent), Wisconsin (33 per cent), and North Carolina (26 per cent) ranked above the national average of 25 per cent; New York coincided with the national average. These four states also ranked above the national average in terms of the proportion of the state's labor force employed in manufacturing. California and New Mexico, despite the rapid rate of growth they showed in manufacturing industry, ranked below the national average in terms of both percentage of individual income payments derived from manufacturing and percentage of employed persons working in manufacturing.[7]

Four of the six states (California, Wisconsin, North Carolina, and New York) are among the nation's top farm states in terms of cash receipts from farm marketings. California's farmers topped the list in 1953, claiming approximately $2.6 million in cash return from farm marketings of both crops and livestock. Wisconsin ranked tenth, North Carolina twelfth, and New York thirteenth. In California's agricultural economy, specialty fruit and vegetable crops are particularly valuable as a source of income. Wisconsin has specialized in dairy agriculture, with increasing emphasis in recent years on non-dairy livestock. North Carolina ranked low in receipts from livestock and related products, but high in receipts from tobacco.[8]

7. *Ibid.*, Table 345, p. 292.
8. *Ibid.*, Table 780, p. 642.

Agriculture did not bulk very large as a source of individual income payments in any of the states, despite the large total cash receipts in four of the states. In 1953 agriculture produced nationally about 5.3 per cent of total individual income payments: North Carolina was above the national average with 12.8 per cent; New Mexico and Wisconsin were also above the national average;[9] the other three states were below average, with New York standing forty-sixth. Thus in three of the six states under study, agriculture may be considered a more significant segment of the economy than it is in the country as a whole. A similar picture is revealed by examining the proportion of the labor supply in these states engaged in agriculture and related industries (including forestry and fisheries): North Carolina, Wisconsin, and New Mexico devote a larger proportion of their manpower to these pursuits than does the country as a whole; California, Connecticut, and New York are well below the national average.[10]

Trade, distribution, and service industries (including government) are of major importance in California and New York. In terms of manpower about two-thirds of the working population in California and about 60 per cent in New York are employed by these industries; the national average is close to one-half. The expansion of such secondary or service enterprises is characteristic of a highly developed industrial economy with high per capita income creating demand for professional, business, and personal services.

Finally, the importance of government in the economy of New Mexico should be noted. Federal, state, and local government salaries provided a quarter of the total individual income payments in the state during 1953, ranking New Mexico second among the forty-eight states in terms of the

9. *Ibid.*, Table 345, p. 292.
10. *Ibid.*, Table 244, p. 210.

proportion of personal income received from government. California and North Carolina also ranked above the national average of 15.9 per cent.

The six states thus include major industrial states and major agricultural states, states with high per capita income and some with relatively low per capita income. They are growing rapidly and reflect the nation's trend towards urban and metropolitan expansion.

THE SIX STATES:

THEIR POLITICAL AND GOVERNMENTAL CHARACTER

Outwardly, the six states display considerable uniformity in governmental structure, as indeed do most of the forty-eight states. All have a popularly elected governor and a bicameral legislature with the rural population and small communities generally over-represented and residents of the major urban centers under-represented. All six states have a large number of local governmental units, running from over 2,500 in New York (excluding school districts) to a low of 108 in New Mexico.[11] In three states (New York, Wisconsin, and California) more such local units exist than in the average state. In addition to counties, municipalities, and townships, these local governmental units include a wide variety of special districts ranging from such interstate units as the Port of New York Authority to such common types as housing, utility, soil conservation, water control, and road districts. Despite these similarities in governmental structure, if one goes behind formal institutions to seek an understanding of how these institutions operate and something of the forces playing upon them, subtle and often important differences among the forty-eight political systems begin to emerge. In the following brief comparison of the six states, emphasis is directed as much to these significant distinctions as to patterns of uniformity.

11. *Ibid.*, Table 455, p. 397.

Party politics in the six states have followed somewhat different patterns, although in five states (all except New Mexico) political alignments have tended to be more or less stable. Two-party competition, though varying in degree of intensity, tends to characterize contemporary politics in the states of California, New York, and Connecticut. In Wisconsin over the last half-century, choice for the voter has tended to be at times within the Republican party and at times between a third party (the La Follette Progressive party) and the Republicans. More recently the trend has been towards a revival of two-party competition between Democrats and Republicans in state as well as in national elections. North Carolina superficially appears to follow the stereotype of the Southern one-party state, yet factional alignments within the dominant Democratic party have been relatively more stable than in many one-party states. As a result North Carolina voters have frequently faced choices among issues rather than simply among competing personalities. In New Mexico politics appear highly personalized despite the appeal to traditional national party labels.[12]

Sectionalism and urban-rural cleavage mark the political struggle in each of the six states. Similarly, agricultural interests are well organized and politically articulate in all. Organized labor is an important political force particularly in New York, Wisconsin, California, and Connecticut. In all six states the lobbying activities of particular business interests are both well organized and well financed. Finally, there have been unique political movements or issues which have

12. For more detailed discussion of state politics in the six states see the following: W. Moscow, *Politics in the Empire State* (New York: A. A. Knopf, 1948); D. G. Farrelly and I. Hinderaker (eds.), *The Politics of California* (New York: Ronald Press, 1951); T. C. Donnelly (ed.), *Rocky Mountain Politics* (Albuquerque: University of New Mexico Press, 1940); C. B. Judah and F. C. Irion, *The 47th State* (Albuquerque: Division of Government Research, University of New Mexico, 1956); and V. O. Key, Jr., *Southern Politics in State and Nation* (New York: A. A. Knopf, 1949), Chapter 10.

stirred individual states. Behind the contemporary politics of Wisconsin, for example, is the story of Joe McCarthy and his meteoric rise; in California there have been the issues of old-age pension politics and tidelands oil.

The character of a state's administration is determined chiefly by the strength of the executive branch. A diagnosis of the executive branch can therefore give insight into the conditions under which scientific programs in the six states are administered. Two related questions are considered: (1) What is the governor's role as chief administrator and chief policy maker? (2) What progress has been made towards developing modern tools of executive management? On the basis of the governor's position as policy leader and directing head of state government, the six states can be readily divided into three groups: the governorship is strongest in New York and California, moderately strong in Wisconsin and Connecticut, and weakest in North Carolina and New Mexico.

In New York and California, states with a strong executive, most major administrative positions are filled by gubernatorial appointment and relatively few department heads are elected. Public administration in these states is highly professional, and the chief executives are probably as well equipped for effective management as is the president of the United States. Both governors enjoy a larger personal administrative staff than the other forty-six governors.[13] They exercise legislative leadership and policy and planning control over state agencies through well developed executive

13. A survey conducted in 1951 revealed that in California the governor's staff included twelve professional assistants, the largest reported for any state. New York's governor reported eleven professional staff aides; the next largest number was seven reported in Michigan. Wisconsin with a staff of six professionals ranked in the next group of states. North Carolina reported a gubernatorial staff of three professional aides and ranked just above the middle in the twenty-five states surveyed. New Mexico's governor had only one professional assistant. C. B. Ransone, Jr., *The Office of Governor in the United States* (University, Alabama: University of Alabama Press, 1956), p. 344.

budget systems covering most state expenditures.[14]   Both states have developed a career service within the framework of a well established merit system governing state employment.   With politics largely eliminated from the classified service, which covers the great majority of state jobs, and with adequate salary levels for most classes, New York and California have been able to compete favorably for public servants with any governmental body in the nation.   The New York and California governors derive further power and influence from their important position in national politics and their recognized role as opinion leaders in large and pivotal states.

New York's governor, in addition to the support he draws from an effective budget staff and a positive program of personnel management, is strengthened by a well integrated state administrative structure.   In contrast to the other five states under examination, New York has moved steadily away from the administrative pattern of vesting in more or less independent boards the authority to supervise administration of important governmental functions.   The organizational chart of California's state government reveals the more normal pattern—a bewildering variety of boards and commissions affiliated in one way or another with virtually every department of state government.   Fortunately for the California governor, departments carrying on major governmental activities are almost invariably headed by single administrators appointed by, and responsible to, the governor.   Furthermore, his management tools, particularly in the areas of budget, personnel, purchasing, and management improvement, enable him to maintain effective control over most of the state administration.

14. The governors' tremendous responsibilities in policy leadership in the big states make effective research an essential staff tool.   As the authors of the New York study point out: "These heavy responsibilities mean that the governor must continuously have studies and programming carried out by experts and specialists dispersed throughout his establishment."   Birkhead and Ahlberg, New York Report, Ch. 1.

In Wisconsin and Connecticut the power of the governor is diluted by a more complicated administrative structure, with more agencies reporting directly to the governor and larger numbers of agencies headed by boards and commissions. Like New York and California, Wisconsin and Connecticut also have well developed state personnel systems based on merit. Indeed, these states have moved even further towards relating personnel management to the governor, Wisconsin by locating its Bureau of Personnel in the Executive Office of the Governor, and Connecticut by designating its state personnel director as one of the governor's principal administrative aides. Both states provide the governor with five to six professional assistants in addition to an executive budget staff and the personnel agency. The Wisconsin budgetary system somewhat limits the governor's fiscal control by assigning him major authority over only the "executive fund budget," which does not include budgets financed out of special funds for state agencies, such as the Highway Department and the Department of Conservation.[15] A governor in Wisconsin or Connecticut, although lacking the well organized and integrated departmental structure of New York or the large staffs of professional assistants and strong budget systems of New York and California, can still become an exceedingly strong chief executive.

North Carolina and New Mexico impose constitutional and statutory provisions upon their governors, significantly weakening their power, prestige, and influence. North Carolina's governor, for example, appears weaker in many ways than his counterpart in any of the other states. He alone of all the American governors is denied the veto power, and he must administer a complex executive establishment composed of 121 state departments and agencies. His power of appointment to important offices is limited and circumscribed; nine state administrative officials besides the governor are

15. Penniman, Wisconsin Report, Ch. 1.

elected. Yet the governor is burdened with making appointments to thirty-six individual positions and to the membership of over one hundred boards and commissions, only a few important enough to warrant his attention. Despite these limitations North Carolina's governors in recent years have tended to be rather successful in giving policy leadership to the legislature and administrative leadership to the departments and agencies. Legislative influence has come primarily from the governor's role as leader of public opinion and from both skill in and careful attention to legislative relations. His success in guiding administration has resulted from aggressive exercise of fiscal control through the executive budget system.[16]

In New Mexico, by contrast, what would appear outwardly to be a strong governorship has become weak through the practice of earmarked funds. With almost 90 per cent of the state's revenue allocated to over two hundred separate funds and with the effective operation of the executive budget system limited largely to agencies financed out of the general fund, the governor's budgetary authority is severely limited.[17] The governor finds his position further circumscribed by the existence of ten other elected executive officials and well over one hundred semi-independent officers and agencies grouped more or less loosely under him. It is little wonder that the phrase "collective leadership" has been used to characterize New Mexico's executive branch of government.[18]

Neither North Carolina nor New Mexico has as yet developed a full-fledged state civil service system, although both are making some progress towards better personnel management. Since 1949 both states have established state person-

16. Cleaveland and Johns, North Carolina Report, Ch. 1.
17. Richards and Radosevich, New Mexico Report, Ch. 1.
18. Judah and Irion, The 47th State, p. 43. On page 44 these authors observe: "A guiding principle of government in New Mexico is its 'fixed fluidity'—that is, affairs are permanently managed on the basis of fluid arrangements among officials operating on an informal basis."

nel agencies and authorized them to undertake classification surveys, to group state positions into defined classes, and to work out uniform pay plans for each class of positions. By the time of this study North Carolina's Department of Personnel had made excellent progress towards classifying the more than twenty thousand positions under the State Personnel Act and had developed pay schedules covering half this number. New Mexico had completed much of the classification job but had not gone far in standardizing salaries. Neither system provides for full application of the merit system with recruitment through open competitive examination and appointment solely on objective qualifications. In both states spoils politics can still be, and sometimes are, pursued.

In summary, the six states represent several points on a scale moving from weak to strong governors. The brief description has emphasized that certain structural elements and management tools are essential to the effective performance of the modern gubernatorial office. The structure of the executive branch, the quality of personnel management, and the adequacy of an executive budget as a means to plan and coordinate state programs are all significant factors affecting scientific activities in the six states.

A NOTE ON AMERICAN FEDERALISM[19]

A study of state governmental activities in the United States should take into consideration the nature of American

19. Material for this discussion is drawn primarily from three sources considered representative of the best informed thinking of recent years on federalism in the United States: The Commission on Intergovernmental Relations, *A Report to the President for Transmittal to Congress* (Washington: Government Printing Office, 1955); W. Anderson, *The Nation and the States, Rivals or Partners?* (Minneapolis: University of Minnesota Press, 1955); and H. C. Mansfield, "The States in the American System," in *The Forty-Eight States: Their Task as Policy Makers and Administrators* (New York: The American Assembly, Columbia University, 1955), pp. 13-39. The Anderson book represents a revision and elaboration of a working paper which Dr. Anderson prepared for the Commission on Intergovernmental Relations, of which he was a member.

federalism, that is, the relation of the states to the central government in this federal union. From the time of the Constitutional Convention in 1787 there has been almost continuous discussion over the nature of the union. The *Report* of the Commission on Intergovernmental Relations in 1955 and the rash of books and articles stimulated by the Commission's study mark another round in this debate. Federalism in the twentieth century has become more than a constitutional and legal theory concerning the allocation of powers and responsibilities. The federal union today is visualized as joining states and central government together in a cooperative, not a competitive, relationship. This relationship is based primarily on shared responsibility for carrying out various governmental programs or services rather than on the claim of exclusive authority by either level of government over these programs.[20]

Associated with this new dimension of public administration added to federalism are several decades of tremendous expansion in the activities of government at all levels in the United States and some significant changes in the nature of these activities.[21] Forty years ago under the impact of World War I the states were emerging from a long period in which their governments had been almost exclusively concerned with the jobs of lawmaking and law enforcement. Now at midcentury the states have moved to the point where, in the words of one observer, they "supplement private resources with the public services and facilities calculated to supply minimum standards of health, shelter, institutional

20. Commission on Intergovernmental Relations, *Report*, p. 68.
21. W. Anderson observes: "If we take expenditures as an index [of the increase in governmental activity] and, putting defense functions and expenditures on one side, consider only non-defense functions within the United States, it is obvious that the states and localities have increased their functions and activities far more than the national government has." *The Nation and the States*, p. 140.

care, recreational opportunities, technical training, mobility; in short the benefits of progress and the blessings of liberty."[22]

This expansion in the activities of state and local governments has come particularly in those areas where state and central government have concurrent responsibilities—areas such as health, education, public works, and agriculture. In this situation, talk about "exclusive" functions and controlling intergovernmental relationships through the principle of functional allocation is hardly realistic. There may be general agreement with the Commission on Intergovernmental Relations on the "main fields of primary National responsibility": "The management of foreign relations in peace and war" (including foreign commitments, defense, control of atomic energy, and internal security); management "of the monetary and credit system"; and "the duty of protecting freedom of trade and facilitating movement and communication within the market place."[23] But even in the case of these broad functions, it is obvious that what the states do may significantly affect national programs and may actually condition what the national government itself can do. In domestic affairs there is much to support Mansfield's conclusion that the role of the states consists of "some part of almost everything, and the whole of very little."[24]

If the principle of functional allocation, then, no longer provides an adequate pattern for intergovernmental relations in many important areas of modern government, what principles are available? The report of the Commission on Intergovernmental Relations and the working paper prepared by William Anderson for the Commission contain some useful ideas. In discussing functional allocation, Anderson notes that there are two methods of administering

22. Mansfield, "The States in the American System," *The Forty-Eight States*, p. 26.
23. Commission on Intergovernmental Relations, *Report*, pp. 62-63.
24. Mansfield, "The States in the American System," *The Forty-Eight States*, p. 25.

governmental programs "intermediate between complete national administration and complete state administration": first, for the state to control and administer the program with financial aid from the federal government and subject to minimum uniform federal standards; and, second, for the total program to be divided into separate activities, some to be carried out by the central government and others to be performed by the state and local governments.[25] These methods suggest two directions which successful programs of joint state-federal action have taken.

At one point in its report the Commission considers the conditions under which the central government is justified in entering as a participant upon service and regulatory activities in which the states are already engaged. The Commission believes that the federal government should participate where there is a need for information and specialized services which are either inavailable or not efficiently utilized unless provided centrally.

Good ideas are likely to be discovered locally on the firing line of practice, but they do not reach fruition unless means exist to clear them centrally and spread them. In addition, much creative thinking is possible only at levels where comparison is feasible or the wider range of relationships is visible.

Finally, certain technical resources, including special equipment and men with specialized training, can sometimes be made generally available only by the National Government. Some of the smaller units are not able to afford or obtain them, and in any case their provision by many units separately would entail costly duplication.[26]

These conditions are likely to occur in conducting scientific activities.

Federal participation is also warranted when financial aid will provide minimum standards of service in the face of

25. Anderson, *The Nation and the States*, p. 144.
26. Commission on Intergovernmental Relations, *Report*, pp. 64-65.

inequalities among the states in fiscal resources. On this point the Commission observes: "The most inclusive areas of government [i.e., the central government] may properly take account of the uneven distribution of local resources when the desirability of universal minimum levels of service is established."[27]

The ideas growing out of the Commission's *Report* and the Anderson book provide at least a beginning for the development of working concepts to help understand patterns of intergovernmental relations in the modern cooperative version of federalism. Since this study is concerned with state scientific activities, it is likewise concerned with intergovernmental relations in the states' scientific effort.

27. *Ibid.*, p. 65.

II

The Scientific Programs

IN THE MID-TWENTIETH century the scientific effort of American state governments has become big business. The scientific programs in each of the six states examined in this study consumed public funds at an annual rate of from $2 million to $32 million.[1] Furthermore, the rate at which state governments are investing scarce funds and skilled manpower in scientific research and development is increasing at a considerable pace. In recent years state governments have stepped up the rate of investment in science and turned more and more to research for solutions to some of their most perplexing problems. Typical of the problems the states are tackling through research are these: how to avoid the staggering burden of institutional care for the mentally ill; how to meet the soaring demand for domestic water supply to sustain the current pace of rapid urban growth and make possible further industrial development in great population centers; how to alleviate the plight of the farmer who in many parts of the nation is still the victim of drought, of pestilence, or of markets flooded with surplus goods. State governments, at times slow to adjust to the rapidly changing environment of the twentieth-century scientific age, are now in the process of catching up, some states moving into ex-

1. The discussion in this chapter is based upon material contained in the six individual state reports prepared for the National Science Foundation. The second chapter in each of these reports sets forth in comprehensive review the total scientific activity program of the state, including an analysis of expenditures for scientific activity, sources of funds, and manpower data.

panded research efforts, other states still cautiously expressing interest in how scientific research may be of help to them.
In examining the scientific programs in the six states
under study, attention will be directed to the place of scientific
effort within the total governmental program of the state and
within various areas of governmental activity, the character
of research performed, the fields of science encompassed, the
sources of financial support, and the investment of professional manpower in scientific activities. This discussion will
place particular emphasis on four areas of governmental activity: agriculture; resource development and public works;
health, education, and welfare; and higher education. Over
85 per cent of all expenditures for scientific activities in each
of the six states were made by governmental agencies operating in these four broad fields, and over 83 per cent of all
the professional personnel involved were employed by these
agencies.[2]

In undertaking this study the basis unit selected for analysis was the scientific activity. The National Science Foundation had already developed the concept of scientific activity
in connection with other surveys for the year 1954 and was
employing this concept in a number of studies including a
survey of federal agencies to determine how they were organized for carrying on scientific work.[3] Accordingly, in

2. In the supporting studies scientific activities in each of the six states
were classified into eight areas of governmental activity: agriculture;
resource development and public works; public safety; business, vocations,
and labor; health, education, and welfare; legislative and judicial research; fiscal and administrative control; and the state university. In
this monograph attention will be focused upon the four major fields of
activity in the interest of simplifying the presentation. The four remaining areas of activity, which have been excluded from consideration here,
are treated in some detail in the six state reports.

3. National Science Foundation, *Organization of the Federal Government for Scientific Activities* (Washington: Government Printing Office,
1956). The glossary in this volume contains formal definitions of the
terms and concepts developed by the Foundation and used by the research
team engaged in this study of state government scientific activities as the
basis for gathering and classifying data. See also National Science Foundation, *Scientific Manpower in the Federal Government, 1954* (Washington:

adopting the scientific activity as the unit for analysis the research team working in the six states hoped that the resulting summaries of data on state government scientific programs might prove comparable to the data emerging from the Foundation studies of the federal government.

The term "scientific activity" as used in this study refers to an activity carried on by a state government agency with the objective of creating new knowledge or of developing new ways or improved ways of applying knowledge to useful purposes. Such activities might involve either the natural sciences (including the life and physical sciences) or the social sciences. On the other hand routine activities designed to meet day-to-day operating responsibilities are specifically excluded even though they may require the use of scientific procedures and skills in their performance.[4]

Scientific activities may include both the actual conduct of research and development and also certain supporting activities which in themselves are not considered research or development. The group of activities classified as research and development will receive more thorough analysis in this study than the other related scientific activities. Research is taken to mean a systematic and intensive investigation having as its object a fuller understanding of the subject under study. Research may be further subdivided into the two categories: (1) basic research which aims at an increase in scientific knowledge as its primary goal; and (2) applied research where the real objective is to make some practical application of the scientific knowledge involved. Development, which is very close to applied research, consists of systematically employing the information and scientific knowledge gained through

National Science Foundation, May 1957) and *Funds for Scientific Activities in the Federal Government, Fiscal Years 1953 and 1954* (Washington: Government Printing Office, 1958).

4. A typical illustration of such routine activities would be the chemical analysis of samples of commercial fertilizers to determine whether they meet minimum standards.

applied and basic research to work towards the production of useful materials, systems, methods or processes but exclusive of design and production engineering.

The related scientific activities include the following: collection of general-purpose data, dissemination of scientific information, training of scientific manpower, planning and administration of research and development, and testing and standardization.

In the discussion which follows the various categories identified above will be employed as tools for analyzing scientific activities. Major emphasis will be given to the conduct of research and development and much less to related scientific activities. Within the category of research and development particular attention will be given to basic research and correspondingly minor attention to development.

TOTAL EXPENDITURES FOR SCIENTIFIC ACTIVITIES

In 1954[5] the six states of California, Connecticut, New Mexico, New York, North Carolina, and Wisconsin expended widely varying amounts on scientific activities, ranging from $2.035 million in New Mexico to $32.297 million in California. Comparison of these figures is almost meaningless; however, when the amount expended on research and related activities is compared to the state's total outlay for general government,[6] the resulting ratio provides a useful standard for analysis (see Table 1). Out of every dollar expended in these six states from $1\frac{1}{4}$ to 2 cents was invested in scientific activities. There is in the six states a pattern of

5. The 1954 data presented in this study are for the fiscal year July 1, 1953, to June 30, 1954.

6. The outlay for general government corresponds to the category of state government general expenditure as used by the United States Bureau of the Census in reporting data on government finance. State general expenditure includes all state expenditure with only two exceptions: liquor store expenditures and insurance trust fund expenditures. See United States Bureau of the Census, *Compendium of State Government Finances in 1954* (Washington: Government Printing Office, 1955), p. 59.

relative emphasis upon research and related scientific activities despite the wide range of absolute amounts expended on these programs.

TABLE I

Total Expenditures for Scientific Activities Compared with Total
Expenditures for General Government in Six States and the
Federal Government (Fiscal Year 1954)

	(a) General Government Expenditures[A] (000)	(b) Scientific Activity Expenditures (000)	(c) b/a (per cent)
California..............	$ 1,682,886[B]	$ 32,297[B]	1.9
Connecticut...........	191,930	2,735	1.4
New Mexico...........	114,922	2,035	1.8
New York.............	1,512,227	18,835	1.2
North Carolina........	391,645	5,806	1.5
Wisconsin.............	357,791	7,151	2.0
Federal Government....	67,772,000	2,072,807	3.0

[A] State expenditure figures are reported exclusive of insurance trust expenditures. The state figures are taken from United States Bureau of the Census, *Compendium of State Government Finances in 1954* (Washington: Government Printing Office, 1955), Table 13, p. 22. The figure for federal budget expenditures for all purposes in the fiscal year 1954 is taken from *The Budget of the United States Government for the Fiscal Year Ending June 30, 1956* (Washington: Government Printing Office, 1955). Public enterprise fund receipts have been excluded from the federal figure.

[B] Exclusive of approximately $55 million expended on federal atomic research administered by the University of California.

When the analysis of spending for scientific activity in relation to spending for all governmental programs is applied to the four major areas of governmental activity, other similarities and some significant differences begin to emerge (Table 2). In every state the proportion of expenditures for general government allocated to scientific programs was larger in agriculture than in any other area of governmental activity. In five states this proportion ranged from one-fifth to two-fifths of the total expenditure; in New York almost two-thirds of the total investment in agriculture went into scientific programs. This proportion is high for at least two reasons. First, the relative importance of research in agriculture is exaggerated by the limited amount the states expended on operating programs in agriculture[7]—less than in the other three fields of governmental activity. The second reason is the important role of agricultural experiment stations in every state in the country. These research agencies, strongly supported by federal aid since the Morrill Act in 1862, represent a rich scientific tradition. The experiment stations have contributed significantly to the development of an agricultural economy based on research. The strong position of research in state agricultural activities is a tribute to the influence of the United States Department of Agriculture, which has stimulated and guided the development of major research efforts in the states through its grant programs and extension service.

In five of the six states the per cent of the total expenditure allocated to scientific activities is smallest in the field of health, education, and welfare (less than 0.5 per cent). In the same way that the agricultural research effort is accentuated by the relatively small amount expended on operating programs, the significance of the health, education, and welfare research effort is partially hidden by the comparatively large expenditures for operating programs. Even the $8.536 million that New York's health, education, and welfare agencies expended on scientific activities in 1954 represented only 1 per cent of the immense $812.9 million budget for all programs in this field.

In the field of resource development and public works four of the states allocated 1 per cent or less to scientific purposes. California and New Mexico, both semi-arid states with major physical resource problems and significant mineral resources, devoted a larger proportion of their expenditures in this area to scientific programs—1.7 per cent and 2.8 per cent, respectively.

7. Operating programs in the field of agriculture tend to be largely the responsibility of the federal government, leaving to the states such functions as inspection and regulation on the one hand, and research service on the other hand.

TABLE 2

Expenditures for Scientific Activities Compared with Expenditures for
General Government by Four Major Areas of Governmental Activity
(Fiscal Year 1954)

	(a) General Government Expenditures[A] (000)	(b) Scientific Activity Expenditures (000)	(c) b/a (per cent)
Agriculture			
California..............	$ 44,829	$ 10,633	23.7
Connecticut............	2,912	1,161	39.9
New Mexico............	2,346	527	22.5
New York..............	7,976	5,221	65.5
North Carolina.........	9,180	2,982	32.5
Wisconsin..............	9,194	3,624	39.4
Federal Government....	2,557,000	49,079	1.9
Resource Development *and Public Works*			
California..............	409,211	6,926	1.7
Connecticut............	48,900	477	0.9
New Mexico............	30,663	873	2.8
New York..............	380,551	1,284	0.3
North Carolina.........	107,035	599	0.5
Wisconsin..............	96,847	923	1.0
Federal Government....	2,824,000	142,185	5.0
Health, Education, and *Welfare*			
California..............	878,482	1,925	0.2
Connecticut............	95,279	341	0.4
New Mexico............	60,766	213	0.4
New York..............	812,949	8,536	1.0
North Carolina.........	202,004	388	0.2
Wisconsin..............	106,903	110	0.1
Federal Government....	2,248,000	114,141	5.0
State University			
California..............	125,959[B]	10,725[B]	8.5
Connecticut............	15,810	467	3.0
New Mexico............	11,503	319	2.8
New York..............	46,228	1,405	3.0
North Carolina.........	39,699	1,586	4.0
Wisconsin..............	39,552	2,280	5.8
Federal Government....	....	....	....

[A] State figures supplied by the staff of the Governments Division of the United States Bureau of the
Census.   These figures are based upon Tables 20 through 25 (pp. 31-37) in the *Compendium of State
Government Finances in 1954.* Federal figures are taken from *Budget of the United States, 1956.*
[B] Does not include approximately $55 million expended on federal atomic research administered by the
University of California.

Four of the states invested 3 to 4 per cent of total expenditures for the state university on scientific activities, chiefly research. Again two states (Wisconsin at 5.8 per cent and California at 8.5 per cent) deviated from the pattern, probably because both these states rely heavily upon their state universities for the provision of major research services.

In all six states the four areas of governmental activity ranked in the same order in terms of total expenditures: health, education, and welfare, first; resource development and public works, second; state university, third; and agriculture, fourth. When the areas are ranked according to the proportion of total expenditure invested in scientific activities, four of the states follow the reverse order: agriculture, first; state university, second; resource development and public works, third; and health, education, and welfare, fourth. In New York the last two areas are transposed; in New Mexico, the state university and resource development and public works received the same proportion. The inverse relationship of course reflects the need for proportionally large expenditures in maintaining the service programs and agencies in the areas of resource development and public works and of health, education, and welfare.

EXPENDITURES FOR CONDUCT OF RESEARCH AND DEVELOPMENT

In the scientific programs each of the six states placed major emphasis upon research. Expenditures for scientific research in 1954 varied from $1.4 million to almost $30 million, representing in five of the states from 70 to 77.5 per cent of the total budget for scientific activity, and in the sixth state (California) over 92 per cent of scientific activity funds. The remaining expenditures for scientific purposes were invested in related and supporting activities, of which the most important was general-purpose data collection. In comparing the nature and scope of scientific programs in the six states, particular emphasis will be placed upon an analysis of expenditures for research and development. Secondary emphasis will be given to the programs for collecting general-purpose data, and brief mention will be made of the remaining scientific activities (scientific information, training of scientific manpower, planning and administration of research, and testing and standardization).

Character of Research

Perhaps the most significant measure of the nature of state scientific activity programs is the analysis of the relative emphasis placed upon basic research, applied studies, and development.[8] Figure 1 shows the distribution of research and development expenditures during 1954 in the six states. In four of the states basic research constituted from one-third to two-fifths of the research and development budget, whereas applied studies accounted for between one-half and two-thirds of the budget. Wisconsin spent approximately one-half of its research budget for basic research while spending correspondingly less than the other states on applied studies. New Mexico allocated only about one-fourth of its research funds for basic investigations and a large proportion on applied studies. Scientific activities properly classed as development were limited in every one of the six states in 1954. Indeed in no one of these states did expenditures for this

8. The same limitation must be noted in connection with the data reported in this survey as has been recorded by the National Science Foundation in its publication presenting data on the scientific effort of the federal government, where the following statement appears: "The problem of classifying research according to whether it is basic or applied and developmental in character is major, since the way in which research is classified depends on a variety of circumstances and judgments which cannot become readily standardized. A further limitation is associated with the fact that basic research which is affiliated with applied or developmental contracts cannot be easily identified from fiscal accounting records, and so has characteristically been underreported. The Foundation is aware of these and similar problems in its reporting of basic research and is making efforts to improve the accuracy of its data." National Science Foundation, *Federal Funds for Science IV, The Federal Research and Development Budget, Fiscal years 1954, 1955, and 1956* (Washington: Government Printing Office, 1955), p. 8.

FIGURE I

DISTRIBUTION OF EXPENDITURES FOR RESEARCH
AND DEVELOPMENT BY CHARACTER OF RESEARCH
(FISCAL YEAR 1954)

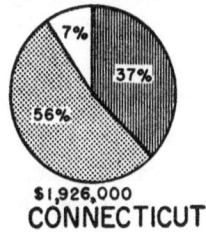

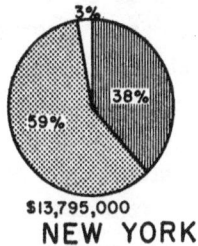

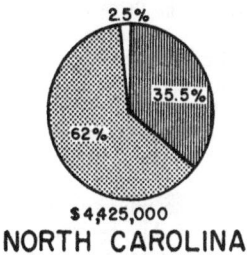

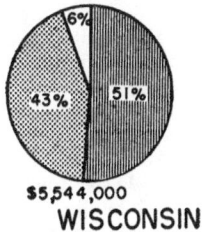

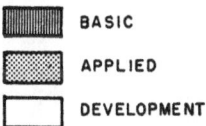

0.5%
35%
64.5%
$29,892,000
CALIFORNIA

7%
37%
56%
$1,926,000
CONNECTICUT

7%
23%
70%
$1,425,000
NEW MEXICO

3%
38%
59%
$13,795,000
NEW YORK

2.5%
35.5%
62%
$4,425,000
NORTH CAROLINA

6%
51%
43%
$5,544,000
WISCONSIN

BASIC

APPLIED

DEVELOPMENT

purpose reach as high as 8 per cent of the funds available for research and development. California, for example, reported less than 1 per cent of its research expenditures allocated to development.

Expenditures for Basic Research.—Expenditures for basic research during 1954 varied from less than $0.5 million in New Mexico to $10.5 million in California. Comparing the six states in terms of the proportion of the total scientific activity budget devoted to basic research, four states spent between one-fourth and one-third of their scientific budgets for this purpose. New Mexico allocated a smaller percentage (16 per cent) and California allocated a larger share (39.5 per cent) to basic research.

All basic research reported was carried on within the four major areas of governmental activity (agriculture; resource development and public works; health, education, and welfare; and higher education). The state university accounted for 50 per cent or more of basic investigations conducted in all states except New York, where the university reported 15 per cent of the basic research expenditures.[9] Again in all

9. The unique organization of public higher education in New York requires brief comment because of its evident effect upon the role of the "state university" in the scientific effort of the state. The State University of New York was established by the legislature in 1948 not as a single educational institution but more as a kind of holding company physically located in the Education Department in Albany and responsible for administering a system of publicly supported institutions totaling by 1954 more than thirty-five separate units. These units included contract state colleges of agriculture, home economics, ceramics, and others attached to private universities like Cornell and Alfred. Also included are new medical schools, four-year liberal arts colleges, and community colleges established by the state in recent years. The relationship between this kind of state system of higher education and scientists employed in state departments and agencies is quite different from that existing in states like Wisconsin and California, for example, where the state university follows a more traditional organizational form. In such states agency heads are likely to turn to their state universities when they want to see certain basic investigations undertaken; in New York by contrast state departments in a comparable situation have more often tended to utilize their own staffs to conduct the studies. This tradition is reflected in the highly developed research facilities and programs of several state agencies. See below, pp. 81-82.

states except New Mexico the agricultural experiment station expended a significant portion of the funds invested in basic research; the New Mexico agricultural experiment station reported no basic research. These two agencies, the university and the agricultural experiment station, accounted for substantially all basic research investment in four states: 100 per cent in North Carolina and Wisconsin; 99.3 per cent in California; and 92 per cent in Connecticut. In New Mexico and New York significant programs of basic research were carried on in agencies outside the state university and the agricultural experiment station.

The New York and New Mexico agencies in question have many of the characteristics of higher educational institutions as instruments for the conduct of research. In New Mexico the Institute of Mining and Technology and the Museum of New Mexico accounted for all basic research conducted outside the state university in 1954. In New York the Roswell Park Memorial Institute and the Psychiatric Institute between them accounted for 42 per cent of the state's basic research expenditures; the university and the agricultural experiment stations expended 45 per cent of New York's basic research funds. The New Mexico Institute of Mining and Technology and New York's Psychiatric Institute both have major teaching and graduate or professional training functions as institutions of higher learning. The Museum of New Mexico is an outgrowth of the School of American Research, its employees are all associates in the School, and its research activities are closely coordinated with the educational programs of the School. New York's Roswell Park Memorial Institute is a largely autonomous medical research laboratory and hospital set up within the Department of Health. The Institute staff is devoted to cancer research and specialized training of advanced medical and dental students.

State governments are relying heavily, and it is likely that they will continue to rely heavily, upon their institutions of higher education to conduct basic research. Such organizations with their detachment from the day-to-day pressures of operating programs are more likely to provide an environment conducive to the performance of basic research.

Expenditures for Applied Research.—Investment in applied research varied among the six states from just under $1 million in New Mexico to over $19 million in California. In four of the states this investment represented from 40 to 50 per cent of the total scientific budget. Wisconsin allocated only one-third of her scientific activity budget to applied research; California allocated about three-fifths of her scientific expenditures for this purpose. Four states spent on applied studies from one-half to two-thirds of their expenditures for research and development; again Wisconsin was below the others, spending 43 per cent, and New Mexico was high, devoting 70 per cent of her research expenditures to applied research (Figure 1).

In each of the six states the agricultural experiment station expended more funds to finance applied research than any other state agency, accounting for approximately half (from 40 to 56 per cent) of the expenditures for applied research in four states and 70 per cent of applied research funds in Wisconsin.[10]

Programs of applied research were distributed rather evenly throughout the major areas of governmental activity. Agencies from all four major areas carried on applied studies. Of the approximately 150 agencies[11] surveyed in the six

10. In New York the two agricultural experiment stations between them put more money into applied research in 1954 than any other single state agency, although the health, education, and welfare agencies as a group expended more on applied studies than the agricultural agencies. The experiment stations accounted for about 30 per cent of New York's total investment in applied research.

11. This figure includes agencies in the four minor areas of governmental activity covered in the individual state reports but excluded from this summary monograph.

states which were carrying on some kind of research activity, 91 per cent of them reported expenditures for applied research. This wide distribution of expenditures for applied studies reflects the use of applied research as a means to support operating programs. Whereas only universities and those state agencies with important characteristics of universities tend to carry on basic research, line agencies in the different fields of governmental activity tend increasingly to look to applied research as a means of solving problems and providing support for their operating programs.

Fields of Science

A second measure of a state's research and development effort is the relative emphases placed upon life, physical, and social sciences. This study suggests that state research efforts are heavily weighted in the direction of life sciences. As Figure 2 indicates, in five of the six states over half the expenditures for research were used to finance work in the life sciences, and none spent less than 40 per cent. Every state but New Mexico invested over $1 million in life science research in 1954, with California spending almost $16 million and New York well over $10 million in this field.

The physical sciences claimed approximately 20 to 30 per cent of the research funds expended by four of the six states during 1954. New York allocated a smaller proportion than the other states, spending 5 per cent of its research funds on studies in the physical sciences, whereas New Mexico allocated to such studies almost half of its research and development expenditures. Expenditures for studies in the social sciences represented from 13 to 20 per cent of the research funds in five states, with Wisconsin spending a substantially smaller proportion.

In sharp contrast, distribution of the federal government's research and development expenditures in the same year was over 87 per cent to the physical sciences, 11 per

FIGURE 2

DISTRIBUTION OF EXPENDITURES FOR RESEARCH
AND DEVELOPMENT BY FIELD OF SCIENCE
(FISCAL YEAR 1954)

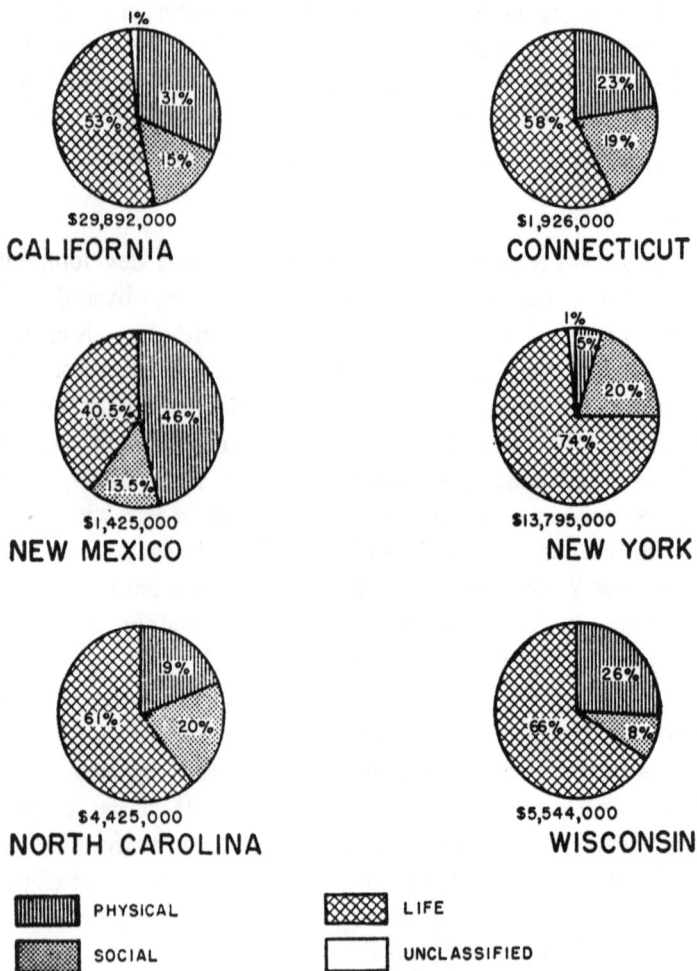

cent to life sciences, and less than 2 per cent to the social sciences.[12] This heavy weighting of federal research work in the physical sciences results quite naturally from the prominent place this field commands in the nation's defense research effort and the large investment of federal research dollars in national security programs.

Expenditures for Life Science Research.—The life science research programs tend to be concentrated in a small number of agencies. The agricultural experiment station is the dominant agency in this field of science. In five states the experiment station expended three-fifths to four-fifths of the funds invested in life science studies. In New York the experiment stations expended approximately one-third of the life science research funds. Four states reported their experiment stations financing studies in the life sciences during 1954 at the rate of $2 million per year, with California reporting slightly more than $9 million. In California, North Carolina, and Wisconsin the state university is the other major agency engaged in conducting life science research.

Only in New York do the state health, education, and welfare agencies account for a substantial proportion of the research carried on in the life sciences. New York's agencies in this area, principally the Departments of Health and Mental Hygiene, reported an expenditure of over $5 million to finance studies in the life sciences, representing approximately half of the state's total investment in life science research in 1954. Health, education, and welfare agencies in all the other five states combined expended just a little more than 10 per cent of the total invested by the New York agencies.

Each of the six states reports some life science research in the area of resource development in connection with the state's responsibility for fish and wildlife conservation. Such

12. These data are taken from National Science Foundation, *Federal Funds for Science IV*, p. 7 and Table 5, p. 28.

research is supported largely by federal grants-in-aid under the Dingell-Johnson and Pittman-Robertson programs of the United States Department of the Interior.

Expenditures for Physical Science Research.—The bulk of the expenditures for research in the physical sciences was reported by the state universities and by the agencies in the area of resource development and public works. The only major exceptions are New York's Departments of Health and Mental Hygiene, which accounted for over 80 per cent of that state's investment in physical science research during 1954. In four states the state universities absorbed approximately 60 to 85 per cent of the funds allocated to studies in the physical sciences. New Mexico's universities (exclusive of the Institute of Mining and Technology) expended about 40 per cent of that state's physical science research dollars.[13] In most of the six states the highway departments were the principal agencies conducting physical science research in the area of resource development and public works. New Mexico and California also reported significant expenditures for their programs of water resource development and utilization and of mineral exploration.

Expenditures for Social Science Research.—In general, the six states reported a lower level of expenditure to finance research in the social sciences than in the case of either life science or physical science research.[14] Only California and

13. State University of New York has been omitted from this discussion because the supporting study reports no physical science research conducted by the University during 1954. When the New York report was in process of reproduction, information was received indicating that the College of Ceramics at Alfred University (a contract college within the State University of New York) had expended $302,000 for physical science research during 1954. These figures were not incorporated into the tables presented in the state study or into the present study. Birkhead and Ahlberg, New York Report, Ch. 9.

14. There are two important exceptions to this observation: (1) North Carolina reported approximately the same expenditure for physical science research as for social science research; (2) New York spent over four times as much on social science research ($2.8 million) as it did on physical science research ($670,000).

New York spent over $1 million on all social science research in 1954 ($4.4 million and $2.8 million respectively). Furthermore, in only one case did state agencies in a single area of governmental operation spend as much as $1 million to finance studies in the social sciences: California's health, education, and welfare agencies, which expended $1.3 million on social science research.

Despite this proportionally lower level of support, in each of the six states social science research tended to be spread widely throughout state government activities. Almost 70 per cent of the state agencies surveyed in the six states which reported expenditures for the conduct of research carried on studies in the social sciences. Every state reported expenditures to finance social science research in its agricultural experiment station, its state university, and its agencies in the fields of health, education, and welfare; three states carried on social science research in the area of resource development and public works as well. This wide participation in social science research activities reflects the concern of state agencies with social phenomena in virtually every phase of governmental operation.

EXPENDITURES FOR RELATED SCIENTIFIC ACTIVITIES

Expenditures in the six states for general-purpose data collection, scientific information, training of scientific manpower, planning and administration of research, and testing and standardization ranged in 1954 from approximately $0.5 million in New Mexico to over $4 million in New York. Four of the six states invested over $1 million in such scientific programs. Comparing these expenditures with total scientific activity spending, five of the states allocated from 20 to 25 per cent of their scientific budgets to these related activities. California devoted only about 7 per cent of its total expenditures for scientific activities to supporting related scientific activities.

Expenditures for General-Purpose Data Collection

In each of the six states the collection of general-purpose data was the second most important scientific activity as measured by dollars invested or by the number of agencies engaged in the activity. Five of the six states invested from one-eighth to one-fourth of their total scientific activity expenditures in the collection of general-purpose data—from approximately $0.5 million to over $2.7 million. California, the sixth state, allocated only about 6 per cent of its scientific budget to data collection, although this investment represented an expenditure of over $2 million in 1954, second in absolute amount only to the New York expenditure. Five of the six states gave heavy emphasis in their data-collection activities to gathering information about social phenomena, spending from two-thirds to nine-tenths of their data-collection funds for this purpose. The sixth state (New Mexico) allocated slightly over one-half of its data-collection funds to resource development and public works agencies for gathering data on physical phenomena.

In each of the six states data-collection activities were scattered through many different agencies in all major areas of governmental activity except the state universities. This wide dispersion of data-gathering activities throughout state governments testifies to the increasing value to operating programs of the collection and scientific analysis of data. The relative importance of data-collection programs in terms of dollars invested also underlines the significant role that state governments are performing as suppliers of basic information about both physical and social phenomena.

Expenditures for Scientific Information

Each of the six states carried on scientific information activities in 1954. Expenditures for this purpose varied from $20,000 in North Carolina to $165,000 in New York and represented in the case of four states less than 1 per cent of their total scientific activity expenditures. New Mexico reported investing slightly less than 2 per cent and Connecticut slightly over 3 per cent of their scientific budgets for scientific information purposes. These expenditures go into such programs as the publication of scientific journals and monographs, the maintenance of small research libraries, and the sponsorship of conferences to disseminate scientific findings.[15]

Expenditures for Training of Scientific Manpower

Four states (Connecticut, New York, North Carolina, and Wisconsin) reported expenditures for the training of scientific manpower during 1954. The amounts invested in these training programs varied from $20,000 in Wisconsin to over $1 million in New York and represented from 0.3 per cent to over 5 per cent of total state scientific activity expenditures. All the agencies reporting expenditures for the training of scientific manpower were located in the area of health, education, and welfare. The training programs tend to be of three kinds. First, health departments, and especially the mental health agencies, have undertaken to provide financial support for programs to train psychiatrists and mental health workers. Secondly, as a means of raising the professional quality and standing of their staffs, departments of public welfare have sponsored programs of educational leave to encourage employees to obtain graduate and professional training. Finally, departments of education have also entered into programs of educational leaves to attain better trained professional staffs.

Expenditures for Planning and Administration of Research

California, Connecticut, New York, and North Carolina have invested small portions of their scientific activity funds

15. Unfortunately, in many cases expenditures for scientific information were not recorded separately in agency accounts, and these costs have therefore been buried in the expenditures reported for research and development. Expenditures for scientific information activities reported in this study are thus understated and the actual investment made by the six states for this purpose is larger than these figures suggest.

in separately organized arrangements for planning and administering research. The expenditure for this purpose in 1954 did not total over $160,000 nor bulk larger than 0.8 per cent of the total scientific activity budget in any of the four states. In two states the agencies reporting such expenditures were in the area of resource development and public works; in the other two states health, education, and welfare agencies accounted for the expenditure.

Expenditures for Testing and Standardization

Only two states (New York and North Carolina) reported expenditures for testing and standardization in 1954. In both states the investment was small ($130,000 and $5,000 respectively) and represented a small fraction of the total scientific activity budget (approximately 0.7 per cent in New York and 0.1 per cent in North Carolina).

SOURCES OF FUNDS EXPENDED IN SCIENTIFIC ACTIVITIES

From one-half to four-fifths of the total scientific activity budgets in the six states came from state government appropriations. In North Carolina and Wisconsin the state's share was roughly one-half; in California, Connecticut, and New Mexico the state contributed approximately two-thirds; and in New York state appropriations made up almost 82 per cent of the state's scientific activity budget. In absolute amounts these state appropriations to scientific activity programs in 1954 ranged from $1.2 million to $22.4 million.

Miscellaneous sources, such as individual and corporate gifts, foundation grants, income from contracts with private corporations, and income from the sale of publications and agricultural produce, provided from 5 to 10 per cent of the funds for financing scientific activities in four of the states. Wisconsin drew 17 per cent of its scientific activity budget from such funds; New Mexico drew only 3.5 per cent of its scientific activity expenditures from miscellaneous sources. Most of the money from these sources went into the two areas of agriculture and the state university, which together accounted for over 95 per cent of such monies in four states. Federal agencies provided support for scientific activities in five of the six states to the extent of one-fourth to one-third of the total expenditure for scientific programs (Table 3, column f). New York drew only about 10 per cent of its scientific activity budget from federal government sources. In two states the federal contribution to scientific programs in 1954 totaled approximately $0.7 million, in three states roughly $2 million, and in California almost $8 million. Although these are large amounts of money and obviously

TABLE 3

Federal Contribution to State Expenditures for General Government
and Scientific Activities Compared with Total State Expenditures
for General Government and Scientific Activities
(Fiscal Year 1954)

| | GENERAL GOVERNMENT EXPENDITURES | | |
	(a) Total (000)	(b) Federal Contribution (000)	(c) b/a (per cent)
California.............	$1,682,886	$254,617	15.1
Connecticut...........	191,930	18,702	9.7
New Mexico...........	114,922	26,541	23.1
New York.............	1,512,227	179,766	11.9
North Carolina........	391,645	61,616	15.7
Wisconsin.............	357,791	57,496	16.0

| | SCIENTIFIC ACTIVITY EXPENDITURES | | | |
	(d) Total (000)	(e) Federal Contribution (000)	(f) e/d (per cent)	(g) e/b (per cent)
California.............	$32,297	$7,940	24.6	3.1
Connecticut...........	2,735	720	26.3	3.8
New Mexico...........	2,035	684	33.6	2.6
New York.............	18,835	1,949	10.3	1.1
North Carolina........	5,806	1,977	34.0	3.2
Wisconsin.............	7,151	2,367	33.1	4.1

significant proportions of the scientific activity budget in each of the six states, they represented only a very small percentage (from 1.1 to 4.1 per cent) of the total federal contribution (Table 3, column g).

The total federal monetary contribution to state expenditures in 1954 ranged from a low of $18.7 million in Connecticut to a high of almost $255 million in California. A more useful basis for comparison lies in the ratio between federal contribution and total state expenditure. In these terms a reasonably clear pattern emerges with federal funds constituting from 12 to 16 per cent of total state expenditures in four of the states. Connecticut derived only about 10 per cent of its total program expenditure from federal sources, whereas New Mexico drew 23 per cent of its total expenditure from federal contributions.

Comparison of column (f) with column (c) in Table 3 suggests that in 1954 the states depended upon the federal government more heavily for the support of scientific programs than for the support of other state government activities. Five of the six states—all but New York—derived between one-fourth and one-third of their scientific activity budgets from federal funds, whereas four of these five drew less than one-sixth of their total expenditures for general government from federal government sources.

In each of the six states federal funds supported scientific programs in all four major areas of governmental activity (Table 4). Two different comparisons are useful in analyzing the distribution of federal funds for scientific activities among these four areas. First, how do the areas compare in terms of dollar amounts of federal support for scientific activities? Second, how do the areas compare in terms of their degree of dependence on federal support for their scientific activities?

As Table 4 shows, in four states the largest dollar volume of federal support of scientific programs went to the state

TABLE 4

Federal Contribution to Scientific Activity Expenditures Compared
with Total Scientific Expenditures by Major Area of Governmental
Activity (Fiscal Year 1954)

	(a) Scientific Activity Expenditures (000)	(b) Federal Contribution (000)	(c) b/a (per cent)
Agriculture			
California..............	$10,633	$ 749	7.1
Connecticut...........	1,161	223	19.2
New Mexico...........	525	162	30.9
New York.............	5,221	414	7.9
North Carolina........	2,982	669	22.4
Wisconsin.............	3,624	597	16.5
Resource Development *and Public Works*			
California..............	6,926	699	10.0
Connecticut...........	447	96	21.4
New Mexico...........	873	309	35.4
New York.............	1,248	473	35.1
North Carolina........	599	104	17.4
Wisconsin.............	923	337	36.5
Health, Education, and *Welfare*			
California..............	1,925	358	18.6
Connecticut...........	341	73	21.4
New Mexico...........	213	11	5.2
New York.............	8,536	381	4.4
North Carolina........	388	144	37.1
Wisconsin.............	110	53	48.2
State University			
California..............	10,725	5,923	55.2
Connecticut...........	467	235	50.3
New Mexico...........	319	168	52.7
New York.............	1,405	301	21.4
North Carolina........	1,586	1,003	63.2
Wisconsin.............	2,280	1,298	56.9

universities and the agricultural agencies (especially the
agricultural experiment stations). In California, Connecticut, North Carolina, and Wisconsin, federal support in these
two areas accounted for 64 to 84 per cent of the total federal
contribution to state scientific activities. By contrast, in New
Mexico and New York the resource development and public

works agencies claimed more federal dollars for scientific programs.

Analysis of the degree of dependence on federal support (Table 4, column c) suggests a pattern among the states. In all but New York the state universities relied more heavily on federal funds for their scientific activity programs than did the other agencies. At the other end of the scale the agricultural agencies ranked last or next to last in terms of degree of dependence on federal sources to finance their scientific activities.[16]

The six states drew considerable federal support for all programs in their health, education, and welfare agencies— $11 million to $181 million. In four states the federal government provided from 20 to 25 per cent of the total state expenditures for health, education, and welfare purposes and in two states, from 12 to 13 per cent. However, the federal contribution to state government scientific research in health, education, and welfare is not impressive. This federal contribution lags behind the federal investment in state university research, the support for agricultural research and related activities, and in five states behind the federal contribution to resource development and public works.[17]

16. It may appear inconsistent to find that the agricultural agencies rank high in terms of the amount of federal support received and low in terms of the degree of dependence on federal support. The reason is, of course, that a relatively large volume of support for agricultural research is provided by the state itself.

17. It is true that some federal funds going to support research in the state university were allocated to research in health carried on in medical schools and teaching hospitals affiliated with the various state universities. In 1954 these funds amounted to approximately $150,000 to $200,000 in New York, North Carolina, and Wisconsin and $925,000 in California. Even if these amounts were added to the federal contribution in that year to regular state agencies for scientific activities in health, education, and welfare, it would not change the picture materially. Still no state would be allocating more than 0.9 per cent of its federal funds for health, education, and welfare to scientific activities. In only one state (New York) would this federal contribution rank higher than third and above the federal support of agriculture and of the state university (less the medical schools).

This pattern of relative dependence upon federal support suggests that the federal government in 1954 was playing a particularly important, though perhaps obscure, role in financing basic research activities at the state level. Thus in four states the state university and the agricultural experiment stations accounted for 92 per cent or more of the total state investment in basic research; in addition, two-thirds or more of the 1954 federal contribution to scientific activity in these states was expended by the universities and agricultural experiment stations. Federal funds were supporting heavily the scientific programs of the very agencies in these four states which gave primary emphasis to basic research. While the data on federal funds contributed to state scientific activity cannot be classified in terms of the character of the research which these funds helped to finance, it would appear a reasonable inference to conclude that in California, Connecticut, North Carolina, and Wisconsin federal funds for scientific activities provided heavy support for basic research programs in 1954.

PROFESSIONAL MANPOWER INVESTED IN SCIENTIFIC ACTIVITIES

Another measure of the scope of state scientific activities and the extent of state support for these programs may be found in the state's manpower investment. In these studies particular attention has been given to the professional personnel carrying on scientific work in state government, the kinds of scientists engaged in this work, the extent of their investment of time, and, where possible, some consideration of their salary levels and status as employees of state government. As part of the over-view of scientific activity programs in the six states a few general comparisons of manpower investment follow. More detailed discussion of scientific manpower in the six states is reserved for a later chapter.

In 1954 the six states reported from 197 to over 3,000 professional personnel engaged in scientific activity programs exclusive of the agricultural experiment stations.[18]   The amount of time these scientists devoted to scientific programs ranged from 131 man-years to over 1,332 man-years.   Four states (Connecticut, New Mexico, North Carolina, and Wisconsin) each reported from about 200 to 600 scientists devoting something less than 300 man-years to scientific activities.   New York reported almost 1,500 professional personnel investing slightly more than 900 man-years, whereas California claimed over 3,000 scientists at work on scientific activities for a cumulative total of 1,332 man-years during 1954.

In terms of the fields of science of the professional personnel,[19] three states (New York, North Carolina, and Wisconsin) reported over half of their scientists in the life sciences, with physical scientists and social scientists each running approximately 20 to 25 per cent of the total. Connecticut and New Mexico reported a larger percentage of physical

18. Analysis of manpower data in the individual state studies has been complicated by the fact that the manpower information furnished by the agricultural experiment stations in several instances was not comparable to that supplied by other state agencies.   In the interests of obtaining manpower summaries for each of the states, which could then be compared, the state study directors were asked only to report the information provided by the experiment stations but not to include these data in their detailed analyses of the professional manpower situation.   Therefore, in this discussion of professional personnel engaged in scientific activities the agricultural experiment stations have been omitted.

19. This comparison is based on classification of the positions occupied by professional personnel engaged in scientific activities in the six states. Official job titles were reported and then classified as belonging in the life sciences, in the physical sciences, or in the social sciences.   There is no necessarily exact correlation between field of science of the position the scientist holds and the field of science of the research in which he is engaged.   Thus life scientists and physical scientists may be collaborating on a research project which is classified as life science research.   Classification of expenditures for research as life, physical, or social science refers to classification of the particular study for which the money was expended and does not necessarily mean that professional individuals from this same field of research were conducting the study.

scientists (from 40 to 48 per cent) than either life or social scientists. In no state did social scientists represent the largest proportion of professional personnel engaged in scientific activities.

In Table 5 the man-year investment and dollar investment in scientific activities are related to obtain the dollar expenditure per man-year in each of the six states during 1954.

TABLE 5

Expenditures for Scientific Activities per Man-Year Invested
(Fiscal Year 1954)

	Total man-years invested^A	Total scientific activity expenditure^A	Expenditure per man-year
California...............	1,332.0	$22,881,000	$17,176
Connecticut.............	148.0	1,610,000	10,878
New Mexico.............	131.4	1,511,000	11,496
New York..............	904.0	13,900,000	15,376
North Carolina..........	275.4	3,704,000	13,449
Wisconsin..............	160.0	3,654,000	22,837

^A Both manpower data and expenditure data for the agricultural experiment stations have been excluded from this table.

The bulk of professional man-years was devoted to research and development, just as the largest expenditures in each state were for research. Five states reported from two-thirds to a little over three-fourths of their man-year investment going to research and, conversely, from one-fourth to one-third to related scientific activities. In California 94 per cent of professional man-years went to research.

This brief discussion of the professional man-years allocated to scientific activities in the six states does not alter the picture of scientific programs sketched earlier through analysis of expenditure data. The states tend to allocate manpower in much the same patterns in which they budget expenditures for scientific activities. Most of the funds and

most of the manpower are invested in research and development.   Most of the research and most of the scientists carrying it on are in the field of the life sciences.   The six states
tended to fall in substantially the same rank order when their
dollar investment in scientific activities is compared as when
their manpower investment in these programs is compared.

III

Scientific Activities in Four Major Areas

THE MATERIAL presented in this chapter is organized around four major areas of governmental activity: agriculture; resource development and public works; health, education, and welfare; and the state university. The primary focus is upon the substantive program of research and development and related scientific activities in each of these fields with some attention to patterns of expenditures in the six states within each area, sources of funds, and the character of the research effort. Again the analysis will be comparative, seeking to call attention to significant similarities and differences among the six states.

DISTRIBUTION OF EXPENDITURES FOR SCIENTIFIC ACTIVITY

In the preceding chapter (Table 2) spending for scientific activities was compared with general expenditures in the four major fields of governmental operation. It was shown that the proportion of total state expenditures devoted to scientific activity was larger in agriculture than in the other three areas of state government. In other fields examined the proportions of state expenditures allocated to scientific work were much smaller, seldom totaling more than 5 per cent.

Another way to determine the relative emphasis given to the different fields is to explore the distribution of scientific activity expenditures in the four areas of governmental activity. The diagrams in Figure 3 indicate little consistency among the six states. Research and related activities in agri-

FIGURE 3

DISTRIBUTION OF EXPENDITURES FOR SCIENTIFIC
ACTIVITIES BY MAJOR AREAS OF GOVERNMENTAL
ACTIVITY (FISCAL YEAR 1954)

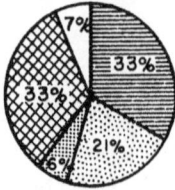

CALIFORNIA

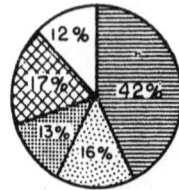

CONNECTICUT

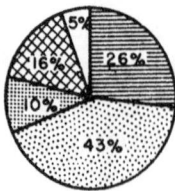

NEW MEXICO

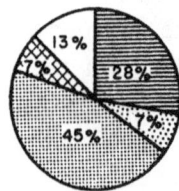

NEW YORK

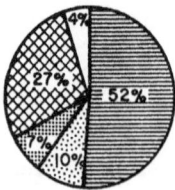

NORTH CAROLINA

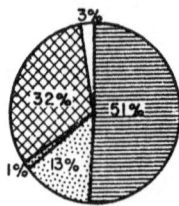

WISCONSIN

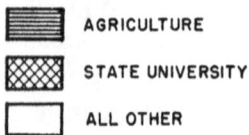

AGRICULTURE

STATE UNIVERSITY

ALL OTHER

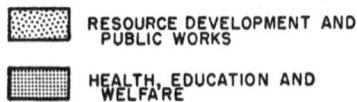

RESOURCE DEVELOPMENT AND
PUBLIC WORKS

HEALTH, EDUCATION AND
WELFARE

culture tended to dominate the scientific budgets of Wisconsin, North Carolina, and Connecticut and to hold an important position in the scientific activity programs of all six states. Resource development and public works activities led the way in New Mexico; health, education, and welfare held first place in New York; and in California the state university received the largest expenditures for scientific purposes. As Figure 3 suggests, of all the six states Connecticut has the most balanced distribution of scientific expenditures, with no one area receiving over half of the scientific activity budget.

Figure 4 represents for each of the states the distribution of expenditures for general government among the four major areas of governmental activity in 1954. The evidence of a generally uniform pattern is quite striking. Five of the six states devoted about one-half of their total expenditures to the fields of health, education, and welfare. All six states invested about one-fourth of their total expenditures in resource development and public works. In five of the states the investment in the state university was about one-tenth of total expenditures. Agriculture received the smallest proportion in all six states, ranging from 0.5 per cent in New York to a high of only 3 per cent in California and Wisconsin.

Why should these six states reflect such a high degree of uniformity in the proportion of their total expenditures allocated to the four areas of governmental activity, and why should the distribution of scientific activity expenditures in the same year suggest so little evidence of pattern? With the differences in the character of the six states, in economic opportunity, in population, in natural resources, and in a host of other elements, the absence of pattern in distribution of scientific activity expenditures is perhaps more understandable than the apparent uniformity in distribution of general expenditures.

FIGURE 4

DISTRIBUTION OF EXPENDITURES FOR GENERAL
GOVERNMENT BY MAJOR AREAS OF GOVERNMENTAL
ACTIVITY (FISCAL YEAR 1954)

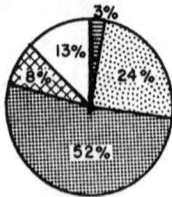

CALIFORNIA

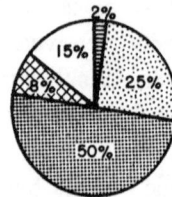

CONNECTICUT

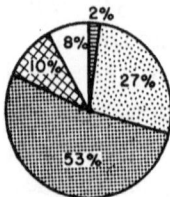

NEW MEXICO

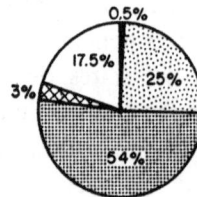

NEW YORK

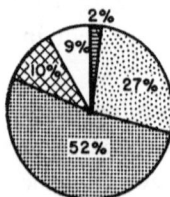

NORTH CAROLINA

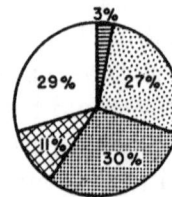

WISCONSIN

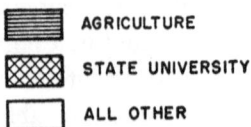

AGRICULTURE

STATE UNIVERSITY

ALL OTHER

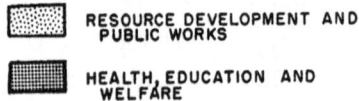

RESOURCE DEVELOPMENT AND PUBLIC WORKS

HEALTH, EDUCATION AND WELFARE

In New York, for example, strong political support from Governor Dewey, the presence of outstanding research scholars in the Departments of Health and Mental Hygiene, and the long tradition of research might account in part for the much higher level of expenditures for scientific activity in the health, education, and welfare area. The unique nature of the state system of higher education in New York might explain the low level of investment in scientific activity within the state university area. The relatively high level of support for scientific activity in the field of resource development in New Mexico may be explained by the critical need of the state for more adequate water supply, as well as by the major importance of the mineral industries in the economy of the state. The high rate of expenditure for agricultural research and related activities in Wisconsin and North Carolina may be accounted for by the strategic importance of agriculture in their economy and by the strong political position of farmers and farm organizations in both states. There is no lack, then, of plausible speculations to explain the distribution of scientific activity expenditures. Why such factors were not also operating to introduce wider variations in the distribution of expenditures for general government is not readily apparent.

AGRICULTURE[1]

Agriculture is a major industry in every one of the states under examination. California, capitalizing on a highly specialized agricultural economy, claims first place among the states in cash income derived from agriculture. Placing particular emphasis upon high value specialty crops, California's farmers have stressed intensive cultivation and su-

1. This discussion is based upon material contained in the following sections of the individual state reports: Marshall, California Report, Ch. 3; Lehmann, Connecticut Report, Ch. 3; Richards and Radosevich, New Mexico Report, Ch. 3; Birkhead and Ahlberg, New York Report, Ch. 4; Cleaveland and Johns, North Carolina Report, Ch. 3; and Penniman, Wisconsin Report, Ch. 3.

perior quality of farm products through research and through well organized producers' associations.

In New York agriculture is still the state's largest industry, particularly strong in poultry raising, vineyard and orchard products, and dairy products. Over half of New York's approximately thirty million acres are devoted to farming, producing wealth that ranks New York thirteenth among the states in total annual value of farm products.

Wisconsin and North Carolina are both heavily engaged in agriculture. Wisconsin's annual cash farm income has topped $1 billion consistently since 1951, with dairy farming contributing approximately half this total income. North Carolina, with its major crops in tobacco and cotton, derives over $900 million annually in cash receipts from agriculture. Moreover, this state has the largest rural farm population of any state in the union.

In New Mexico agriculture yields about one-seventh of the total income produced in the state, even though only about 1.5 million acres out of 4 million acres of arable soil can be farmed consistently. Even in highly industrialized Connecticut, where the dependence upon agriculture might appear to be relatively minor, farm lands under cultivation are valued at over $300 million and annual cash income from farming totals over $1 million. Furthermore, Connecticut boasts the first agricultural experiment station in the country.

It is apparent, then, that the governments in all six states have good reason to support extensive research seeking a more prosperous agriculture.

Expenditures for Scientific Activity

In dollar terms four of the states invested between $3 million and $10 million in agricultural research and related activities in 1954. Only Connecticut with $1 million and New Mexico with $0.5 million fell below. In relative terms two states (Wisconsin and North Carolina) devoted over one-half of their scientific budgets to agriculture; the next two states invested from one-third (California) to two-fifths (Connecticut) of their total scientific activity expenditures; and the remaining two states (New York and New Mexico) allocated to the area of agriculture approximately one-fourth of all they spent on scientific activities. The share of the expenditures agriculture claimed for research is even more impressive. Three of the six states (North Carolina, Wisconsin, and Connecticut) spent about one-half of all the funds they invested in research on studies in the area of agriculture; the remaining three states spent about one-third of their research funds for studies in agriculture. This heavy emphasis upon agricultural research in the scientific programs of all six states reflects the strong position of leadership in research exercised by the agricultural experiment stations.

Another measure attesting to the great interest of state legislatures in agricultural research may be found in the relatively high level of appropriations for agriculture in 1954. It is not federal support, although this is not inconsequential, but rather state appropriations that make possible extensive scientific activity programs in the field of agriculture. In four of the six states appropriations for scientific work were larger in agriculture than in any other field of governmental activity.[2] In the other two states (New York and New Mexico) about a quarter of what was appropriated for scientific activity went into agriculture.

All six states drew their major support for scientific work in agriculture from state appropriations. In five states (all but New Mexico) over two-thirds of the scientific budget for agriculture came from state sources. In these same five states the federal contribution, although moderately impressive as dollar figures (ranging from $223,000 to $748,000

2. In North Carolina and Wisconsin two-thirds of all the funds appropriated for scientific activity in 1954 went into the field of agriculture. In California and Connecticut 42 per cent of total state appropriations for scientific work were devoted to agriculture.

in 1954), represented only from 7 to 22 per cent of the total invested in agricultural scientific activities. New Mexico provided 57 per cent of the total expenditures for scientific work in agriculture from state appropriations and received federal support to the extent of 31 per cent of the total.

Expenditures for Conduct of Research and Development.—Figure 5 shows the distribution of agricultural research expenditures by character of research. A rather clear pattern emerges from the figure. Five of the states allocated from one-fourth to one-third of their agricultural research dollars to basic research and from three-fifths to three-fourths of these dollars to applied research. New Mexico devoted all of its agricultural funds to applied studies. With the exception of some research conducted by the California Department of Agriculture, all the basic research in agriculture in the six states was carried on by the various state agricultural experiment stations. These stations also conducted nearly all applied research studies in four of the states and approximately 93 per cent of these studies in California. Only in North Carolina was a substantial part of the applied research expenditure (30 per cent) made by an agency other than the agricultural experiment station.[3]

The agricultural research programs in 1954 also followed a fairly standard pattern in the relative emphasis given to the fields of science (Figure 6). Life sciences accounted for 83 per cent or more of agricultural research funds in all six states. Two states reported no physical science research expenditures in agriculture, and no state reported more than 6 per cent of its agricultural research funds invested in physi-

3. In North Carolina the state Department of Agriculture operates the test farms at which the scientists of the agricultural experiment station carry out their controlled experiments. In many cases, therefore, the costs of animals, fertilizers, seed, and labor used in applied research work are charged to the Department of Agriculture rather than to the experiment station. Cleaveland and Johns, *North Carolina Report*, Ch. 3.

FIGURE 5

DISTRIBUTION OF EXPENDITURES FOR RESEARCH AND
DEVELOPMENT IN AGRICULTURE BY CHARACTER OF
RESEARCH (FISCAL YEAR 1954)

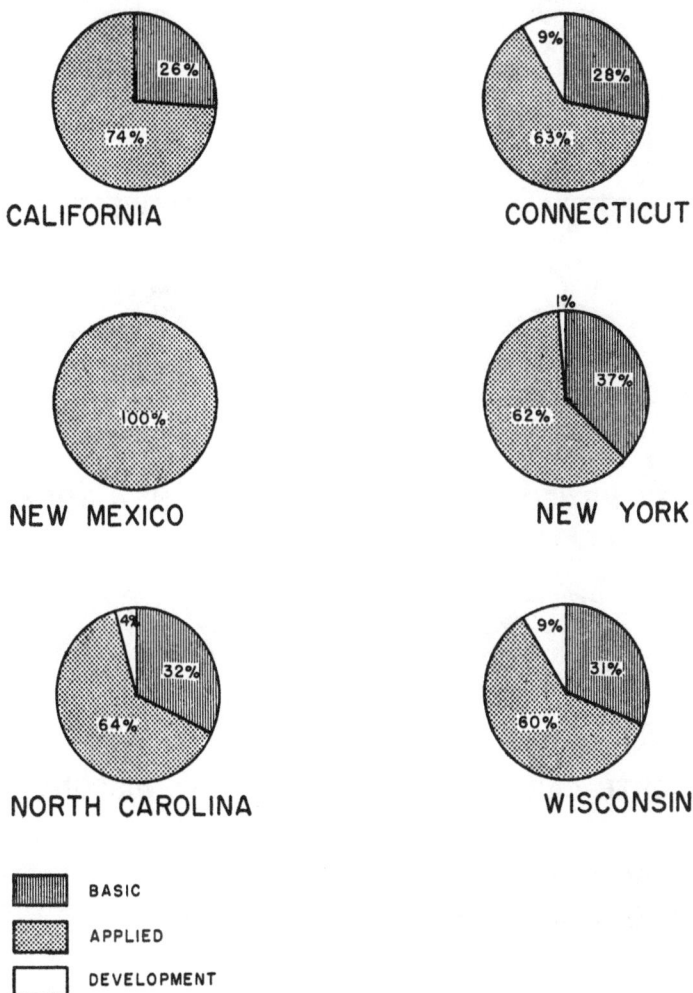

CALIFORNIA

CONNECTICUT

NEW MEXICO

NEW YORK

NORTH CAROLINA

WISCONSIN

▓ BASIC
▒ APPLIED
☐ DEVELOPMENT

FIGURE 6

DISTRIBUTION OF EXPENDITURES FOR RESEARCH AND
DEVELOPMENT IN AGRICULTURE BY FIELD OF SCIENCE
(FISCAL YEAR 1954)

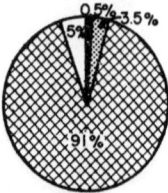

CALIFORNIA

CONNECTICUT

NEW MEXICO

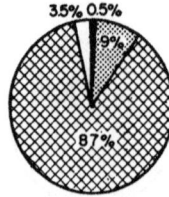

NEW YORK

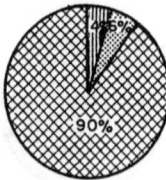

NORTH CAROLINA

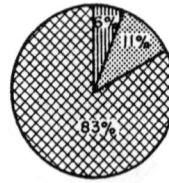

WISCONSIN

 PHYSICAL    LIFE

SOCIAL   UNCLASSIFIED

cal science studies. Every state reported some social science research in its agricultural research program, but social science studies claimed only from about 4 to 11 per cent of the agricultural research budgets.

Expenditures for Related Scientific Activities.—Related scientific activities were of relatively minor importance during 1954 in the agricultural scientific programs in the six states. Five of the states reported expenditures of 3 to 6 per cent of their total agricultural scientific activity budgets for the collection of general-purpose data on social phenomena. There were small expenditures also for scientific information reported by the agricultural experiment stations in New York and Connecticut and by the Department of Agriculture in Wisconsin.[4]

Research Agencies and Their Programs

The agricultural experiment stations are not only the most important agencies carrying on scientific activity in the field of agriculture, but they are among the most important research agencies in all of state government, as measured by the scope of their programs.

In most cases the experiment station is organized as part of the state college of agriculture[5] and conducts its research

4. The report form on which the agricultural experiment stations reported their scientific activity expenditures required a breakdown into only two categories: expenditures for conduct of research and development; and expenditures for other scientific functions. It is not possible in most cases, therefore, to report the allocation of expenditures for related scientific activities to a specific activity, as can be done for the majority of agencies which reported on a different form.

5. Connecticut and New York have two experiment stations each. In New York one station is located at Geneva and the other at Ithaca, and both are considered part of the State College of Agriculture at Cornell University. In Connecticut one is located at Storrs as part of the University of Connecticut College of Agriculture. The second, called the Connecticut Agricultural Experiment Station, is located in New Haven and was at one time affiliated with Yale University. Now it is an independent station cooperating with the Storrs station but retaining its autonomy as a research agency. Birkhead and Ahlberg, New York Report, Ch. 4; and Lehmann, Connecticut Report, Ch. 3.

programs through subject-matter departments set up to correspond with the departments of instruction in the college. These research organizations carry on a variety of projects, some continuing over long periods of time and others begun and completed within a single growing season. In the typical experiment station much of the research is conducted on test, or experimental, farms located in various parts of the state representing different physical conditions such as soil types, topography, rainfall, and altitude. Other research is conducted in laboratories at the station headquarters. In an average year each of the experiment stations is engaged in conducting scores of different projects. In 1954, for example, the New Mexico station reported some 150 projects under way, and the Cornell station had over 500 projects in various stages of completion. A brief annotated listing of the projects undertaken at the California experiment station in 1950 filled a volume of 287 pages.[6]

An experiment station's research program thus defies easy description. Illustrative of the diversity and range of the projects and research interests of a single experiment station is the following statement about the program of the Cornell experiment station at Ithaca, New York, made by its director, C. F. F. Guterman: "The projects receiving attention . . . fall within the general fields of crop and animal production and utilization, protection from diseases and insect pests, marketing and distribution of farm products, costs of production, farm management, conservation of natural resources, and economic and social problems of rural life."[7] Although most of the experiment stations examined in this report pursue studies in a large number of fields as suggested by this statement on the Cornell station, nevertheless their research programs reflect certain primary emphases related to

6. University of California, College of Agriculture, *Research Program of the Experiment Station, 1950-1951* (Berkeley: College of Agriculture, n.d.).
7. Quoted in Birkhead and Ahlberg, New York Report, Ch. 4.

the particular problems of the state's agricultural economy. For instance, the California station devoted about 20 per cent of its expenditures in 1954 to studies related to horticultural crop production. Research in this same field dominated the program of the Geneva station in New York and ranked high on the program in North Carolina. Studies in field crop production, botany and plant pathology, and soils and plant nutrition claimed major emphasis in the programs of stations in North Carolina, New Mexico, and Connecticut. Wisconsin's station gave particular stress to research on the processing and marketing of food products, especially dairy products. Experiment stations in all six states devoted major attention to research on animal production; these studies absorbed 26 per cent of the Connecticut station's research funds, 16 per cent of the California station's funds, and 17 per cent of the North Carolina station's budget. In the case of every station a careful scrutiny of the relative percentage of funds allocated to particular groups of studies suggests much about the character of the agricultural economy in the state, the major concerns of its farmers, the interests of the station's scientists, and the comparative strength of various agricultural interests in the state.

The agricultural experiment stations are not the only state agencies engaged in scientific activities in the field of agriculture. In each of the six states there was at least one other agency active in this field. The state departments of agriculture in all except New Mexico were engaged in some form of scientific activity in 1954. For the most part these agencies are responsible for carrying on service and regulatory programs to support the agricultural industry in their states. They collect and disseminate various kinds of information on marketing conditions, price quotations, crop and livestock estimates, weather data, and the like. The agricultural statistics divisions of these departments serve as the state units cooperating in the Joint Federal-State Crop and Livestock

Reporting Service. The state departments of agriculture also are responsible for insect and pest control programs; inspection of seeds, animal feeds, and fertilizers; and quality control programs seeking to improve the standards of various crops produced and marketed in their states. These activities involve a variety of data-collection programs and in some states incidental research studies. Typically, research undertaken by a state department of agriculture tends to be applied, seeking to solve problems arising in the course of regular operating programs.

In a number of the states there are also special crop or product organizations that carry on scientific activities. Connecticut's Milk Administrator, the California Poultry Improvement Association, and the New Mexico Sheep Sanitary Board are illustrative of these organizations. Some are primarily engaged in regulatory work seeking to protect producers, distributors, and consumers by exercising controls over such matters as processing, handling, and pricing commodities. Others are essentially quasi-public trade associations seeking to promote producers' interests through developing better strains of product and upgrading quality going to market. In this context the California industry advisory boards deserve special mention. Although largely autonomous agencies organized within specific product groups (the Cling Peach Advisory Board, the Wine Advisory Board, and the Dairy Industry Advisory Board are illustrations), these advisory boards are officially associated with the California Department of Agriculture. They share responsibility with the Department for the administration of various marketing order programs designed to safeguard producers and handlers from loss resulting from disorderly and unsound marketing conditions. These programs are financed by assessments charged to growers and handlers. In 1954 collections from the combined thirty or more industry groups represented by advisory boards totaled more than $7 million annually. The various advisory boards allocated approximately $327,000 of these funds to finance research designed to improve product quality and increase market demand. Customarily the boards conduct little research through their own staffs but rather contract with various research agencies (public or private) to carry on the studies, often calling on university scientific facilities both inside and outside the state. This device of the advisory boards appears to afford a particularly useful opportunity for government officials and private producers to cooperate closely in the development of effective programs to promote better agricultural marketing through research and education, as well as through regulation.[8]

RESOURCE DEVELOPMENT AND PUBLIC WORKS[9]

Unlike the field of agriculture where one major research agency has tended to dominate scientific activities, the area of resource development and public works was reported to have four to six agencies carrying on important scientific work in each of the six states. These agencies can be classified into two categories: conservation or natural resource agencies; and public works agencies, for the most part highway departments. Four of the states have developed more or less comprehensive departments of conservation, combining in a single organization concern for development and effective utilization of a variety of natural resources. These agencies differ somewhat in scope. For example, in both California and North Carolina fish and wildlife resources are the responsibility of a separate organization, whereas agencies concerned with parks, forests, and minerals are

8. Marshall, California Report, Ch. 3.
9. This discussion is based upon material contained in the following sections of the individual state reports: Marshall, California Report, Ch. 4; Lehmann, Connecticut Report, Ch. 4; Richards and Radosevich, New Mexico Report, Ch. 3; Birkhead and Ahlberg, New York Report, Ch. 5; Cleaveland and Johns, North Carolina Report, Ch. 4; and Penniman, Wisconsin Report, Ch. 4.

housed together in a single department. North Carolina also includes water resource development in this department, but California places this responsibility in a department of public works along with the state highway division. New York and Wisconsin group responsibility for fish and wildlife, forestry, and parks within their departments of conservation. New York also adds responsibility for water resource development to this agency; Wisconsin does not. New Mexico and Connecticut have separate agencies for fish and wildlife, water resources, geological investigation, and highways.

Expenditures for Scientific Activity

Resource development and public works activities claimed second place as a consumer of state expenditures in 1954. Each of the six states devoted about a quarter of its total expenditures to this field of governmental activity, a larger share than that invested in any other area of governmental service except for health, education, and welfare. In terms of scientific activity expenditures, four of the states invested from 10 to 20 per cent of their scientific budgets in resource development and public works, placing this area third after agriculture and the state university as a consumer of scientific activity dollars. New Mexico expended 43 per cent of its scientific budget for these activities, more than it spent on scientific work in any other area during 1954. The remaining state (New York) allocated only about 7 per cent of its scientific funds to resource development and public works. In dollar amounts the expenditures on scientific research and related activities in this field ranged from slightly below $0.5 million to almost $7 million.

The federal government has demonstrated major interest in this field as expressed through grant-in-aid programs and other devices to encourage state initiative. Such federal agencies as the Forest Service, the Geological Survey, and the Fish and Wildlife Service maintain extensive cooperative relations with state officials concerned with resource utilization problems. Similar relationships also exist in the highway programs where the Bureau of Public Roads supports and assists state highway departments in the planning, construction, and maintenance of interstate highways. These cooperative relationships are further buttressed by significant federal financial support. In 1954 three states derived about one-third of their total scientific budget for resource development and public works from federal contributions; in two states the federal contribution ran somewhat lower at about 20 per cent; the sixth state (California) received about 10 per cent from federal sources. State appropriations thus accounted for two-thirds to four-fifths of the funds invested in this field during 1954.

Expenditures for Conduct of Research and Development. —There is a more even distribution of funds between the conduct of research and related scientific activities in the area of resource development and public works than in any of the other three major areas of governmental activity. The pattern of distribution, however, followed no consistent lines in 1954 over the six states. Five states varied from spending one-third of their funds for research and two-thirds for related work to exactly the reverse ratio. The sixth state (California) devoted 83 per cent of its scientific budget for resource development and public works to research and development and 17 per cent to related scientific activities.

As Figure 7 reveals, every state expended most of its research funds in resource development and public works on applied research. Correspondingly, little money was allocated in any of the six states to either basic research or development. Three states (New Mexico, New York, and Connecticut) invested from 4 to 6 per cent of their research funds in basic research studies, all conducted by educational

FIGURE 7

DISTRIBUTION OF EXPENDITURES FOR RESEARCH AND
DEVELOPMENT IN RESOURCE DEVELOPMENT AND
PUBLIC WORKS BY CHARACTER OF RESEARCH
(FISCAL YEAR 1954)

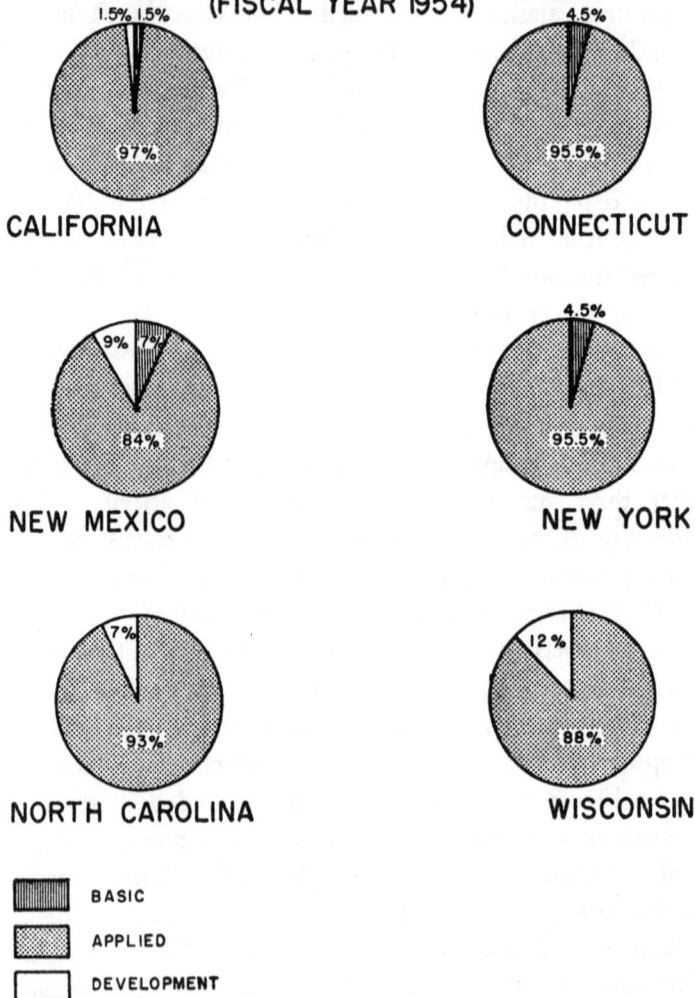

1.5% 1.5%

97%

CALIFORNIA

4.5%

95.5%

CONNECTICUT

9% 7%

84%

NEW MEXICO

4.5%

95.5%

NEW YORK

7%

93%

NORTH CAROLINA

12%

88%

WISCONSIN

BASIC

APPLIED

DEVELOPMENT

agencies.[10] Again, three states (Wisconsin, North Carolina, and New Mexico) allocated from 7 to 12 per cent of their research funds to developmental studies.

Although the character of the research programs carried on by the resource development and public works agencies was thus quite uniform in the six states, the fields of science receiving major emphasis varied widely (Figure 8). New York and Wisconsin gave heavy stress to studies in the life sciences; California and New Mexico emphasized the physical sciences; and Connecticut and North Carolina devoted most attention to social science.[11]

Possible explanation of this variation in research programs can be found by an analysis of the particular agencies with principal responsibility for resource development and public works. In Wisconsin and New York a large share (87 and 73 per cent respectively) of the research funds in this field was expended by the states' departments of conservation on wildlife, fishery, and forestry research. These studies, all in the life sciences, heavily outweighed the relatively moderate physical science research expenditures by the highway agencies in the two states.

In California and New Mexico, the two states emphasizing physical science research, about 70 per cent of the research funds were expended by agencies responsible for water resource development, mineralogical explorations, and high-

10. These agencies were: the New Mexico Institute of Mining and Technology, which performs both research and graduate training functions; the New York Museum and Science Service, located in the state Department of Education; and the Connecticut Geological and Natural History Survey, dedicated to the conduct of basic research and the publication of results as a means to educate the people of the state.

11. North Carolina and Connecticut did not follow exactly the same pattern in distributing their research expenditures by field of science in this area of resource development and public works. While both states expended 47 per cent of these research funds on social studies, Connecticut expended 44 per cent on physical science research and only 9 per cent on life science studies. North Carolina, on the other hand, devoted about 40 per cent to life science research and only 13 per cent to studies in the physical sciences.

FIGURE 8

DISTRIBUTION OF EXPENDITURES FOR RESEARCH AND
DEVELOPMENT IN RESOURCE DEVELOPMENT AND
PUBLIC WORKS BY FIELD OF SCIENCE (FISCAL
YEAR 1954)

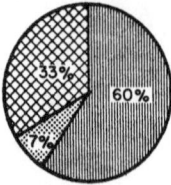

CALIFORNIA

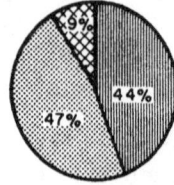

CONNECTICUT

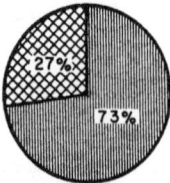

NEW MEXICO

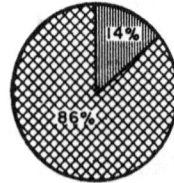

NEW YORK

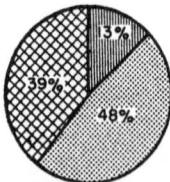

NORTH CAROLINA

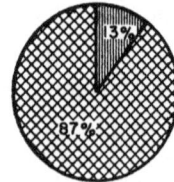

WISCONSIN

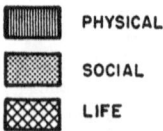

PHYSICAL

SOCIAL

LIFE

way planning and design. Thus the research programs in these states reflect two vital concerns: the serious need for full development and effective utilization of water resources; and the economic opportunity presented by mineral wealth.

In their resource development and public works programs North Carolina and Connecticut gave major place to social science research in two areas: economic development of the state and the planning and financing of highway improvements. Connecticut's Development Commission and Highway Department accounted for 47 per cent of the expenditures; in North Carolina the Department of Conservation and Development, the Highway Commission, and the Institute of Fisheries Research similarly accounted for 47 per cent, all of it going into social science research.[12]

Expenditures for Related Scientific Activities.—As noted above, expenditures for related scientific activities make up a larger share of total scientific spending in resource development and public works than in any other area. In two states, for example (New York and Wisconsin), two-thirds of the dollars spent on scientific work went into scientific activities other than research. Connecticut allocated one-half, and North Carolina and New Mexico one-third each, to related scientific activities. In California the resource and works agencies devoted only 17 per cent of their scientific funds to such activities.

12. This pattern of expenditures in North Carolina is probably not a normal pattern. Three special research studies specifically authorized by the legislature and contracted to outside research organizations contributed a major share of the total research expenditure for 1954. All three studies involved the application of social science analysis to three problems facing the state: economic development of the coastal area through the inland waterway; the economics of the fisheries industry; and the analysis of highway needs and exploration of alternative ways to finance a program of highway construction and maintenance to meet these needs. In a more typical year North Carolina might well have been classified with those states placing major emphasis upon life science research in their resource development and public works programs. Cleaveland and Johns, North Carolina Report, Ch. 4.

More expenditures for general-purpose data collection were reported by natural resources and public works agencies than by agencies in any other field of governmental activity. Only in North Carolina did this field not rank first in expenditures for data collection.[13] In New Mexico and Wisconsin two-thirds of all funds spent on general-purpose data collection in 1954 were accounted for by resource development and public works agencies. In California and Connecticut the fraction was one-half, and in New York and North Carolina 20 to 30 per cent of the total data-collection funds were spent in this area. In five states the development and works agencies gave heavy emphasis to collecting natural phenomena data in 1954, spending from 60 to 100 per cent of their data-collection funds for this purpose. Wisconsin expended 90 per cent of its data-collection funds for information on social phenomena.

State highway departments in all six states carry on important and continuing programs of gathering data, usually on both social and natural phenomena. The following are typical subjects on which these agencies seek to collect data: accidents as related to highway characteristics, volume and speed of traffic at certain points, origin and destination of certain traffic, truck loadings, conditions of highway surfaces, highway costs in relation to revenues, probable yields from types of taxation proposed, and patterns of motor vehicle use.

A representative list of agencies other than highway departments engaged in significant programs of data collection include the following: the water resources agencies (data on stream flow, quality of water, pollution, and ground water), wildlife agencies (surveys of game and fish populations), geological survey agencies (data on mineral location, geologic formations, oil and gas pools), and economic development agencies.

13. In North Carolina agricultural agencies and those in health, education, and welfare reported larger expenditures for data collection during 1954.

Resource development and public works agencies in five of the states (all except North Carolina) reported modest expenditures for scientific information in 1954, ranging from 1 to 7 per cent of the amount invested in related scientific activities (or from about $8,000 to $44,000). With the exception of a small expenditure made by the Wisconsin Highway Commission, all the scientific information activities were reported by agencies concerned with development of natural resources.

North Carolina and California agencies in resource development and public works also devoted some of their scientific activity funds to the planning and administration of research. In both states these were the only instances reported in this study where agencies allocated funds to this purpose. The California expenditure totaled $159,000 and represented 13 per cent of the expenditures for related scientific activities in the resource development and public works field. Although the comparable expenditure in North Carolina was only $44,000, it constituted almost one-fourth of related scientific activity spending by development and works agencies in 1954.

North Carolina also reported a minor expenditure of $5,000 for testing and standardization made by the Minerals Research Laboratory. Only one other expenditure for this purpose was reported in all six states during 1954.

Perhaps the most interesting characteristic of the scientific activity programs in the area of resource development and public works is the variety of agencies engaged in the programs. By contrast, scientific programs in the field of agriculture tend to be dominated by one kind of agency, the line research agency whose major purpose is research. Among resource development and public works agencies engaged in important scientific work, there are at least three different kinds: (1) line research agencies (Connecticut's Geological and Natural History Survey, New York's Museum and Science Service, North Carolina's Institute of Fisheries Research); (2) line fact-finding and trouble-shooting agencies employing scientific activities as a means to facilitate operating programs by solving problems (the fish and game department in each state, the materials and research section, or laboratory, of the highway department in several states); and (3) staff agencies employing research and data analysis as the basis for planning agency operating programs (the planning and research units in several state highway departments).

The close personal collaboration among federal field officials and state scientists in the planning and execution of research and data-collection programs both in the field of natural resources and in highway programs affords a good illustration of cooperative federalism in action. Of course, this federal interest and this kind of collaboration are not unique to the area of resource development and public works; indeed, there are other areas in which the federal government provides both larger funds and a larger share of the expenditures for state scientific activities. Nevertheless, evidence in this study suggests that a closer working relationship exists among federal scientists and state scientists participating in these resource development and highway programs than is true in any other group of programs covered.

HEALTH, EDUCATION, AND WELFARE[14]

Probably no field of state government endeavor has undergone such rapid growth and development in the last decade as has the field of health, education, and welfare. The impact of the Great Depression and then World War II, the explosive growth of our great urban centers, the faster

14. This discussion is based upon material contained in the following sections of the individual state reports: Marshall, California Report, Ch. 6; Lehmann, Connecticut Report, Ch. 6; Richards and Radosevich, New Mexico Report, Ch. 3; Birkhead and Ahlberg, New York Report, Ch. 7; Cleaveland and Johns, North Carolina Report, Ch. 6; and Penniman, Wisconsin Report, Ch. 6.

and faster pace of modern industrial civilization—all these have placed great burdens upon government for health services, for public education, and for public welfare services. The problems of institutional care for those suffering mental illness is itself staggering, let alone the problem of adequate treatment and cure. The character of the schoolroom and teacher shortage in the face of the forthcoming boom in school-age population is such a wide concern of the American public and governmental officials that elaboration is unnecessary.

The proportional allocation of expenditures by state governments to programs in the area of health, education, and welfare testifies to the gravity of these problems and expresses the concern of state governments for them. In five of the six states under examination over half of total expenditures for general government in 1954 were accounted for by agencies operating in this field. The sixth state (Wisconsin) devoted 30 per cent of its total expenditures to these purposes. Table 2 (page 26) indicates that in terms of dollar amounts the investment in health, education, and welfare in these states ranged from about $60.8 million to $878.5 million. Yet a very small part of these large expenditures was devoted to scientific activity programs, running from a low of 0.1 per cent to a high of only 1.0 per cent. In dollar amounts the expenditures involved were from $110,000 to a high of $8.5 million. Only in New York did the area of health, education, and welfare claim first place in expenditures for scientific activities. This state allocated approximately 45 per cent of its total scientific activity budget to agencies in this field. In the other five states this area ranked fourth out of the four major areas of governmental activity in terms of the percentage of scientific activity expenditures accounted for in 1954. These five states spent only between 1.0 per cent and 12.5 per cent of their scientific budgets for such purposes. Indeed, New York state alone expended almost three times as much on scientific activities in the area of health, education, and welfare as the combined expenditure of the other five states.[15]

Expenditures for Scientific Activity

Distribution of scientific activity expenditures between research and development and related scientific activities did not follow any particular pattern in the six states in 1954. Four states allocated 50 per cent or more of health, education, and welfare scientific funds to conduct of research, ranging from 57 per cent in Wisconsin to 95 per cent in California, whereas two states (North Carolina and New Mexico) devoted less than 50 per cent (19 and 42 per cent respectively) of these funds to research. In dollar figures these expenditures for research varied from $63,000 in Wisconsin to $6.6 million in New York, with only two states (New York and California) spending over $1 million and only three states (Connecticut added) spending over $100,000 on research. Again, the New York expenditure amounts to almost three times the combined expenditures for research in the other five states. This research investment represented almost half of New York's total expenditure for research in all fields of governmental activity during 1954. By comparison, the investment in health, education, and welfare research in North Carolina and Wisconsin represented only 1 to 2 per cent of total expenditures for research; in California and New Mexico it amounted to 6 per cent; and in Connecticut, 11 per cent.

15. This comparison of the percentage of scientific activity expenditures allocated to the area of health, education, and welfare in each state is subject to distortion which accentuates somewhat the difference between New York and certain of the other states. Several of the states, including California, Wisconsin, New York, and North Carolina, have developed research programs in the health and mental health fields carried on in the laboratories and teaching hospitals of the state university medical schools. Expenditures for research carried on within such institutions would be classified as scientific activity expenditures in the state university area. Where identical research was carried on in a state health department laboratory it would be classified in the health, education, and welfare area.

As in the case of scientific activities in both the agricultural and the resource development and public works fields, agencies drew major financial support for their scientific work in health, education, and welfare from state appropriations. These state funds supplied 80 per cent or more of the scientific expenditures for health, education, and welfare purposes in four of the states and about 50 to 60 per cent in Wisconsin and North Carolina. Most of the remaining funds used for these purposes came from the federal government. The federal contribution to scientific activities in the area of health, education, and welfare thus ranged from approximately 5 to 20 per cent in four states; it was 37 per cent in North Carolina and almost 50 per cent in Wisconsin. In actual dollars this federal support varied from $11,000 to approximately $381,000.

Expenditures for Conduct of Research and Development. —The distribution of research funds in the six states by character of research is shown in Figure 9. Three states (California, North Carolina, and Wisconsin) put all or nearly all research funds into applied studies, whereas the other three states allocated a significant portion to both applied research and basic research. These proportions represent significant amounts of money only in the case of New York and California. Three states spent less than $100,000 each and a fourth state only a little over $200,000 on research in health, education, and welfare.

The distribution of research funds in this area by field of science follows no clear patterns of emphasis (Figure 10). Life science research dominated the studies conducted by the agencies in New York and Connecticut. The other four states devoted most of their research dollars to social science. North Carolina and Wisconsin expended no funds on physical science research, whereas the other states put a small percentage of their research money into studies in the physical sciences.

FIGURE 9

DISTRIBUTION OF EXPENDITURES FOR RESEARCH AND
DEVELOPMENT IN HEALTH, EDUCATION AND WELFARE
BY CHARACTER OF RESEARCH (FISCAL YEAR 1954)

CALIFORNIA

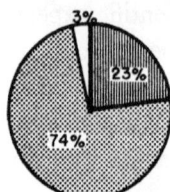

CONNECTICUT

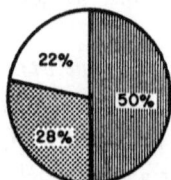

NEW MEXICO

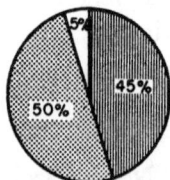

NEW YORK

NORTH CAROLINA

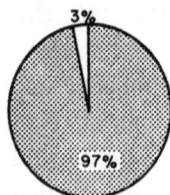

WISCONSIN

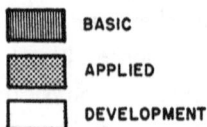

BASIC

APPLIED

DEVELOPMENT

FIGURE 10

DISTRIBUTION OF EXPENDITURES FOR RESEARCH AND
DEVELOPMENT IN HEALTH, EDUCATION AND WELFARE
BY FIELD OF SCIENCE (FISCAL YEAR 1954)

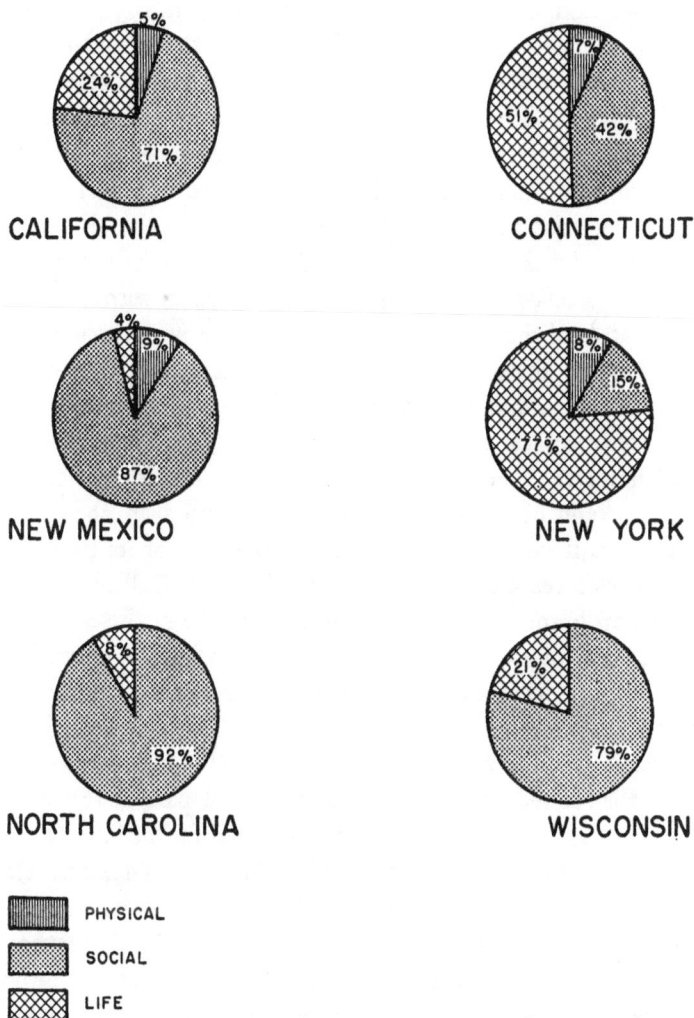

CALIFORNIA

CONNECTICUT

NEW MEXICO

NEW YORK

NORTH CAROLINA

WISCONSIN

PHYSICAL

SOCIAL

LIFE

As noted earlier in connection with the research programs in resource development and public works, variations in expenditures by field of science are likely to be related to the particular kinds of agencies active in the research programs. Thus in New York, Connecticut, and California the health agencies dominated the research programs in 1954. These health agencies accounted for between two-thirds and 95 per cent of all the expenditures for research in health, education, and welfare. The major portion of this research was in the life sciences. In Wisconsin, North Carolina, and New Mexico, education and welfare agencies expended from 70 to 90 per cent of the funds invested in research. Research carried on by these agencies tended to employ the techniques of social science analysis and to be concerned with the subject matter of the social sciences. California provides a major exception to these generalizations. In that state the health agencies accounted for two-thirds of health, education, and welfare research expenditures in 1954, but the principal health agency (the Department of Public Health) allocated 56 per cent of its research funds to studies in the social sciences and expended only about 36 per cent of its funds on life science research. As a result, although California's research program in 1954 was dominated by the health agencies, 71 per cent of expenditures for research in health, education, and welfare went for social science studies and only 24 per cent for life science research.

Expenditures for Related Scientific Activities.—Expenditures for related activities were a significant part of the scientific program in health, education, and welfare in four of the six states. These states (North Carolina, New Mexico, Wisconsin, and Connecticut) devoted from 40 to 80 per cent of their health, education, and welfare scientific funds to these other activities, emphasizing data collection, scientific information, and the training of scientific manpower. By contrast New York and California allocated about 20 per cent and

5 per cent, respectively, of their scientific activity funds for expenditure on related scientific activities. All six states reported expenditures for data collection and for scientific information in 1954, and four states reported important programs designed to train scientific manpower. All the data-gathering programs were concerned with data on social phenomena, with the exception of the New York Department of Health program to which $48,000 was allocated for collecting data on natural phenomena.

The area of health, education, and welfare was the only area in which all six of the states reported expenditures for scientific information programs in 1954. In North Carolina and New York substantially all the expenditures for this purpose were accounted for by health or education agencies. In three other states (Wisconsin, New Mexico, and California) from one-third to one-half of all expenditures for scientific information purposes were reported by the health, education, and welfare agencies.

The training of scientific manpower was also an important element in the scientific activities of these agencies in four states. Three of these (New York, North Carolina, and Wisconsin) reported expenditures for the training of scientific manpower only in the fields of health, education, and welfare. Allocations to these training programs ranged from $20,000 to over $1 million in the four states and constituted between one-third and one-half of the total expenditures for related scientific activities in the fields of health, education, and welfare. Three states reported residency programs for training doctors in clinical psychology, psychiatry, and neurology. Two states have worked out arrangements for granting educational leaves and scholarship aid to certain types of professional personnel enabling them to return to universities for advanced training. Both such programs reported were in the field of public welfare.

Connecticut and New York reported small expenditures for planning and administration of research in the area of health, education, and welfare. The total expenditure involved was small—$8,000 in Connecticut and $65,000 in New York. In both states these were the only instances reported of funds expended for this purpose. In both states these expenditures were made by health and mental health agencies.

Highlights in the Scientific Programs

More individual state agencies were engaged in carrying out scientific activities in health, education, and welfare during 1954 than in any other area of governmental activity. Thirteen different New York agencies were so engaged, ten in North Carolina, seven each in California, Connecticut, and New Mexico, and six in Wisconsin. Broadly speaking, in every state's scientific program in health, education, and welfare major attention was given to the analysis of statistical data as a base for more effective planning of operating programs. This kind of activity was found in nearly all state departments of health, education (or public instruction), and welfare. In four of the states (North Carolina, New Mexico, Wisconsin, and Connecticut) the substantial emphasis in these scientific programs during 1954 was upon data gathering and research based upon statistical analysis. New York and California also gave considerable attention to such work, but placed emphasis upon research not so directly tied to operations and not so rooted in statistical analysis.

The 1954 research program of health, education, and welfare agencies in any of the six states provides illustrations of orientation towards operations. The Division of Public Assistance in Wisconsin's Department of Public Welfare, for example, was engaged in a variety of studies on the characteristics of old-age assistance recipients, analyzing such things as needs, income and resources, insurance holdings, support by responsible relatives, and special characteristics of those receiving blind aid. Connecticut's Community Health Services Division in the Department of Health was studying the relation of socio-economic factors and premature infants in an effort to determine the extent of financial burden on Connecticut's families with premature infants. Another example is the "Stockton Pilot Study" of California's Department of Mental Hygiene. "This was a controlled investigation of the effects of increased staff and intensive treatment on the recovery of chronic schizophrenic patients. ... The experiment was conceived as a bold effort to determine whether the state could save money in the long run by substantially increasing expenditures per patient in the short run."[16] An illustration from the field of education is the study of turnover, loss, and mobility of North Carolina's public school teachers carried on by that state's Department of Public Instruction.

Two of New York's agencies in these fields merit brief consideration because of the national significance of their research programs: the Department of Health and the Department of Mental Hygiene. New York's Health Department expended a little over $5 million on scientific activity programs in 1954, or more than one and a half times the combined expenditures for health, education, and welfare purposes of the other five states. Little wonder that the Department has attained the top position of research leadership among state health departments throughout the country. Perhaps the most significant single element in the program is the work of the Roswell Park Memorial Institute, the state's center for cancer research, administered as a part of the Department's Division of Medical Services. Roswell Park alone expended over $3 million in 1954 on research and training of scientific manpower. Its research program, conducted in conjunction with a 516-bed hospital completed

16. Marshall, California Report, Ch. 6.

in late 1954, gave special emphasis to basic research in physics, biochemistry, and experimental biology. The training program was designed to provide the fourth year of specialist training in therapeutic radiology, anesthesiology, and general surgery.

The New York Department of Mental Hygiene also has developed an impressive program of scientific activities financed at the rate of $2 million annually in 1954. This Department devoted a larger proportion of its research funds to basic research than any other agency in New York state government, largely working through its major agency for research and training, the Psychiatric Institute. Finally, the Department also carries on significant scientific information activities. It publishes *Psychiatric Quarterly,* one of the major journals in the field of psychiatry, and maintains a distinguished scientific library containing such important special collections as the personal library of Sigmund Freud. These two departments alone entitle New York state to recognition as a leader among the states in the conduct of scientific research and related programs.[17]

Even with these major expenditures on research and related scientific activities in the Health and Mental Hygiene Departments, however, New York state in 1954 was allocating to scientific work only 1 per cent of its total expenditures in the area of health, education, and welfare. The other five states in the same period were spending on scientific activities from 0.1 to 0.4 per cent of their total expenditures on health, education, and welfare programs.

State allocation of the large federal contributions to health, education, and welfare activities reveals a similar

17. Birkhead and Ahlberg, New York Report, Ch. 7. It is interesting to speculate on how much the development of research institutions within the framework of state government—institutions like the Roswell Park Memorial Institute and the Psychiatric Institute—can be traced to the absence in New York until recent years of a state university in the traditional sense, with its medical school and its teaching hospital.

pattern. Federal grants received by the six states for these purposes in 1954 represented from 46 to 71 per cent of all the revenue they received from the federal government. Only a tiny portion of these federal grants, between 0.1 and 0.7 per cent, was expended on scientific activities. The unusually heavy outlays made by state governments to carry on large-scale operating and institutional programs in the health, education, and welfare fields, financed out of large state appropriations and major grants from the federal government, seem to dwarf the expenditures for scientific activity in these fields.

This pattern of expenditure allocation in the area of health, education, and welfare contrasts strikingly with the pattern in the field of agriculture.[18] In 1954, for example, the six states spent considerably less on agricultural activities, investing from 0.5 to 2.7 per cent of total state expenditures for this purpose. During the same period the six states allocated to the support of health, education, and welfare activities from 30 to 54 per cent of their total expenditures. Five out of the six states (excluding only New York), however, gave much greater support to scientific activities in agriculture than to similar work in the health, education, and welfare fields. In 1954 they spent from 26 to 52 cents out of every scientific activity dollar on programs in agriculture, while allocating to health, education, and welfare scientific programs from 1 to 13 cents.

It is beyond the scope of this study to do more than speculate briefly on causal factors which may lie behind these expenditure patterns. In the case of agriculture it is likely that the strong support these states give to research is related to the political strength of farmer organizations and the over-representation of rural areas in the state legislatures. Furthermore, state governments generally have become involved to only a limited extent in the costly operating programs in

18. See above, pp. 24-26, 42-45.

agriculture which have developed over the last quarter century as the responsibility of the federal government. This more limited involvement permits the states to continue devoting major attention to providing research services to agriculture. It is more difficult to find possible reasons for the much more limited support five of the six states have given to research in the fields of health, education, and welfare. Perhaps the staggering costs of financing operating programs of institutional care and construction programs for schools, hospitals, and custodial institutions have in effect closed out any real opportunity for the state governments to devote significant proportions of their funds to research in these fields. Perhaps agencies in the health, education, and welfare areas are not properly staffed and equipped to carry on expanded research programs. Indeed, there may be in some of these agencies a tradition of emphasis upon regulatory activities which tends to inhibit the development of greater interests and program in research. With the current rate of growth in the incidence of mental illness and the implications for costly custodial care and treatment, plus the financial burdens of public school expansion, state governments may conceivably face bankruptcy before they can devise adequate solutions to these critical problems through research. Clearly, state and federal policies governing the support of research in this area need sober re-evaluation.

THE STATE UNIVERSITIES[19]

A broadly based system of public education has long been acclaimed as one of America's most significant contributions to modern society, and the state universities of the country constitute the capstone of that system. As institutions of

19. This discussion is based upon material contained in the following sections of the individual state reports: Marshall, California Report, Ch. 8; Lehmann, Connecticut Report, Ch. 8; Richards and Radosevich, New Mexico Report, Ch. 3; Birkhead and Ahlberg, New York Report, Ch. 9; Cleaveland and Johns, North Carolina Report, Ch. 8; and Penniman, Wisconsin Report, Ch. 8.

higher learning their twofold purpose is to provide education and training for the youth of the nation and to contribute in an important way to the search for new knowledge. These twin objectives are indeed inseparable: part of the training and education of youth lies in introducing them into the search for knowledge; and, on the other hand, through this process of the mature scholar and eager student working together comes the fruitful collaboration of creative minds. These two objectives, however, help to make the state university quite a different kind of agency from the more traditional state government bureau with its relatively well defined objectives of providing certain services or regulating certain activities in the public interest. Like the agricultural experiment station, the university is more nearly a line research organization, at least in the sense that research is conducted largely as an end in itself and not because it provides a means to the attainment of some operational goal. The research environment provided by the university campus is also likely to differ considerably from the environment of the typical state department, where operating activities claim the major attention of officials.

The state universities in these six states afforded a varied cross-section of state institutions of higher learning. Included in this group is the largest state university in the nation (the University of California), with eight different campuses throughout the state organized as a unified institution under a single administration. Also included are the oldest state university (the University of North Carolina, which admitted its first students in 1795) and some of the most recently established state institutions of higher education. The State University of New York, for example, was established in 1948 as a corporate entity; it brings together component institutions which date far back in history (the

State College of Agriculture at Cornell) as well as some that were set up quite recently such as the Upstate and the Downstate Medical Centers. Among the universities of these six states are institutions that have provided central intellectual leadership to the people of the state in certain periods[20] and institutions which have tended to be overshadowed by the great private universities within their states.

As an object of expenditure by state government these state universities generally ranked third after the areas of health, education, and welfare and resource development and public works. Three of the states (Wisconsin, North Carolina, and New Mexico) allocated to the universities approximately 10 per cent of their expenditures for general government in 1954. California and Connecticut spent about 8 per cent of their total expenditures and New York about 3 per cent on these state institutions of higher learning. However, the universities received a larger share of the state's scientific activity expenditures than of the state's expenditures for general government. In 1954 the universities claimed about one-third of the scientific activity budgets of their states in California and Wisconsin, about 27 per cent in North Carolina, about 17 per cent in Connecticut and New Mexico, and about 7 per cent in New York. The state university ranked second after the area of agriculture in terms of the proportion of total state expenditure devoted to scientific activity (Table 2, page 26). It is also interesting to note that among the six states under examination, the three whose state universities have won the greatest public recognition as centers for research and graduate training (California, Wisconsin, and North Carolina) tended to rank higher than the other states in terms of the proportion of total university expenditures allocated to scientific activity purposes.

20. For instance, "The Wisconsin Idea." Penniman, Wisconsin Report, Ch. 8.

Expenditures for Conduct of Research

All the scientific activity expenditures reported by state universities in this study were invested in research.[21] In Wisconsin, North Carolina, and California the university research programs in 1954 accounted for 36 to 40 per cent of the total expenditure for research. In Connecticut and New Mexico the university programs represented just under one-fourth of the total research budget, and in New York the state university system accounted for approximately 10 per cent of all the research expenditures. When it is remembered that the agricultural experiment stations are in every case but one (the New Haven station in Connecticut) a part of the state university complex, the major status of the universities as research agencies becomes even more apparent. If the experiment station research expenditures are combined with the expenditures of the state university in each state, the resulting totals constitute over half the total research investment in five of the six states. The only exception is New York, where these combined experiment-station–university expenditures represent only 40 per cent of total expenditures for research. North Carolina and Wisconsin each spent on these educational research institutions approximately 90 per cent of their total research expenditures in 1954; Connecticut spent three-fourths of its research funds; and California, slightly over two-thirds.

Character and Fields of Research in Universities

The strategic importance of these university research programs stands out clearly when the emphasis on basic research is examined (Figure 11). As noted earlier, in five of the six states (excluding New York) the state university

21. The questionnaire employed by the National Foundation to collect data on the scientific activities of colleges and universities contained no questions about related scientific activities. Thus in the case of the state universities the information available for this study is limited to data on expenditures for research and development.

accounted for more than half of the total expenditures for basic research in 1954.[22]   Universities in California, Connecticut, New Mexico, and Wisconsin devoted three-fourths or more of their research funds to basic research.   In New York and North Carolina the corresponding proportion allocated to basic research was 57 and 52 per cent, respectively. Correspondingly, applied research undertakings claimed the largest proportion of expenditures in North Carolina (48 per cent) and New York (43 per cent), whereas these activities were of lesser importance in the remaining four states.

With one exception, the state universities allocated a larger proportion of their research funds to physical science research in 1954 than to studies in other fields of science (Figure 12).   Aside from New York, the proportion of university research funds expended on the physical sciences ranged from a high of 78 per cent in New Mexico to a low of 45 per cent in North Carolina.   Studies in the life sciences ranked in second place as a consumer of university research funds in four of the six states and claimed first place (82 per cent) in New York.   Social science research stood in third place, varying from 27 per cent of university research expenditures in North Carolina to 2.5 per cent in Wisconsin. The pre-eminent position of the universities in the conduct of physical science research has been mentioned earlier.[23]   At this point it is necessary only to recall that during 1954 the universities accounted for about 85 per cent of the total expenditures on physical science research in Wisconsin and North Carolina, over three-fourths in Connecticut, and over 60 per cent in California.

Sources of Funds for University Research

In contrast to the pattern of financing scientific activities in the other areas of governmental activity largely out of

22. See above, pp. 30-32, for a discussion of the university and agricultural experiment station dominance of expenditures for basic research.
23. See p. 36 for a brief discussion of the role of the state universities in the conduct of physical science research during 1954.

FIGURE II

DISTRIBUTION OF EXPENDITURES FOR RESEARCH AND
DEVELOPMENT IN THE STATE UNIVERSITY BY
CHARACTER OF RESEARCH (FISCAL YEAR 1954)

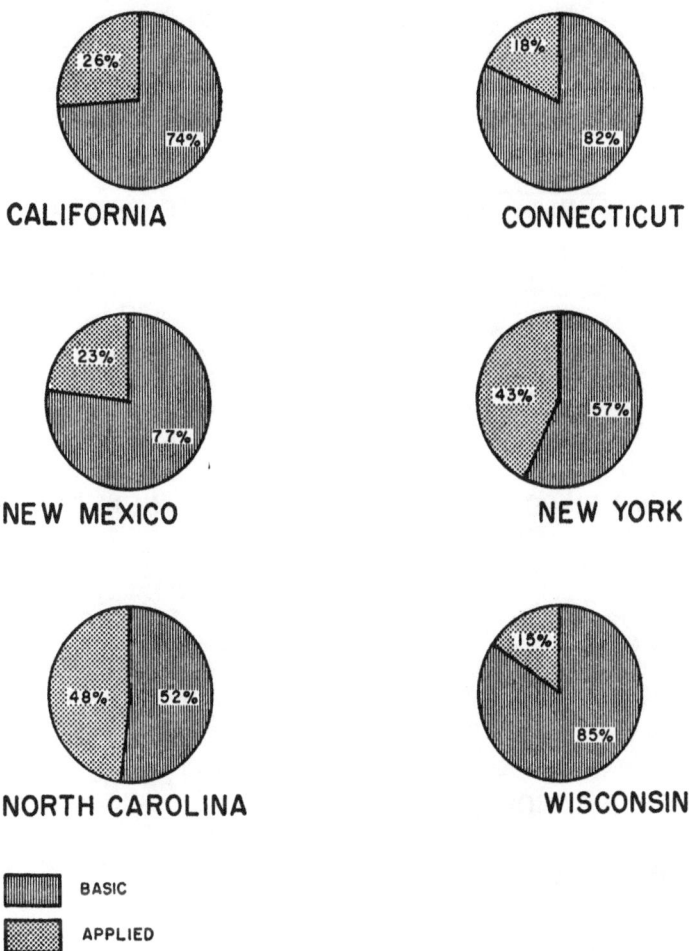

FIGURE 12

DISTRIBUTION OF EXPENDITURES FOR RESEARCH AND
DEVELOPMENT IN THE STATE UNIVERSITY BY
FIELD OF SCIENCE (FISCAL YEAR 1954)

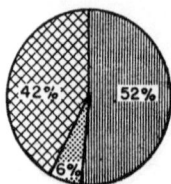

CALIFORNIA

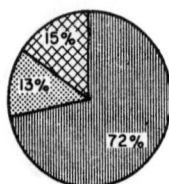

CONNECTICUT

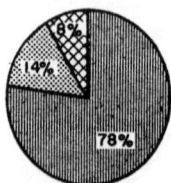

NEW MEXICO

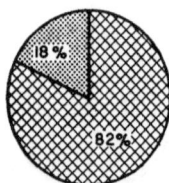

NEW YORK

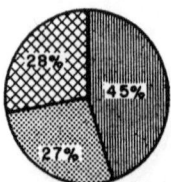

NORTH CAROLINA

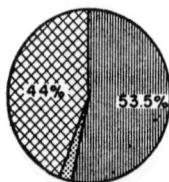

WISCONSIN

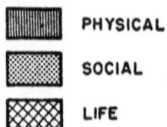

PHYSICAL

SOCIAL

LIFE

state appropriations, in only one of the six states (New York) were such appropriations the largest source of research funds for the state university. The other five states drew 50 per cent or more of their funds for university research from the federal government. The proportion ranged from a high of 63 per cent in North Carolina to an even 50 per cent in Connecticut. Foundation grants, contracts with corporations, private gifts, and other miscellaneous sources of funds furnished a significant part of the financial support for research in the state universities of four states. In Wisconsin these sources provided 25 per cent of the university's research dollars, in New York and North Carolina approximately 18 per cent each, and in California about 10 per cent. State appropriations financed university research expenditures in 1954 at the rate of 60 per cent in New York, 46 to 48 per cent in New Mexico and Connecticut, 34 per cent in California, and 18 to 19 per cent in North Carolina and Wisconsin.

Another measure of the degree of federal government support for state university research may be found in the proportion of federal scientific activity dollars which were expended by the universities. In California three-fourths of all federal dollars contributed to scientific activities in 1954 were expended by the University of California. The state universities in North Carolina and Wisconsin claimed slightly over one-half of the federal dollars contributed to support state scientific activities. In Connecticut the corresponding fraction was one-third, in New Mexico one-fourth, and in New York between one-sixth and one-seventh.

The University Research Programs

Partly because of the nature of universities as research organizations, and partly because of the kind of information this study has gathered on university scientific activities, it is not possible to discuss research programs in this area in the same manner that they have been discussed in other areas of governmental activity.[24]   However, the distribution of research expenditures among the particular schools and colleges engaged in research may provide some clues concerning the nature of these research programs.   Table 6 summarizes this information.

Clearly, the greater proportion of the research, as measured by research expenditures, was carried on in the liberal

TABLE 6

Per Cent Distribution of Expenditures for Research in State Universities
by Schools, Colleges, and Separate Organizations
(Fiscal Year 1954)

	Colleges of Arts and Sciences	Medical and Related Colleges[A]	Schools of Engineering	Separate Research Organizations	Colleges of Agriculture	Other
California.........	45.0	25.0	19.0	10.0[B]	....	1.0
Connecticut.......	81.0	1.0	18.0	....	....	....
New Mexico.......	49.0	....	3.0	38.0[C]	....	10.0[F]
New York.........	....	33.0	....	....	49.0	18.0[G]
North Carolina.....	19.5	24.0	41.0	15.0[D]	....	0.5[F]
Wisconsin.........	75.0	15.5	6.0	3.5[E]	....	....

[A] Includes colleges of medicine, dentistry, pharmacy, and public health.
[B] Represents twenty-two different research organizations.
[C] The Physical Science Laboratory at the New Mexico College of Agriculture and Mechanic Arts.
[D] The Institute for Research in Social Science.
[E] Represents the Laboratory of Experimental Psychology, the Enzyme Institute, and the Engineering Experiment Station.
[F] College of Business Administration.
[G] The School of Industrial and Labor Relations at Cornell University.

24. Statistical data on state university scientific activities were derived from the National Science Foundation's study of institutional research. These data were obtained from university business offices through mailed questionnaires.   This questionnaire is reproduced in National Science Foundation, *Scientific Research and Development in Colleges and Universities, Expenditures and Manpower, 1953-54* (Washington: Government Printing Office, 1958), Appendix C, pp. 130-50. Generally in this survey of state scientific activity, university scientists were not interviewed concerning their specific research projects in the same manner as state agency personnel had been interviewed.   Interviews conducted with university officials and faculty members were designed to gather information about the general role of the university as a research agency and not about specific research undertakings.

arts departments of the state universities. Thus, in 1954 the college of arts and sciences accounted for 81 per cent of university research expenditures in Connecticut, three-fourths of the total in Wisconsin, and almost one-half in California and New Mexico. The major exception is New York, where the liberal arts colleges of the state university system did not report any research. In North Carolina these colleges expended only one-fifth of the total university research budget for the year. Medical colleges claimed second place in four states, reporting one-third of total university research expenditures in New York, about one-fourth in California and North Carolina, and 15 per cent in Wisconsin. Schools of engineering accounted for about two-fifths of the university's total research expenditure in North Carolina, about one-fifth in California and Connecticut, and 6 per cent in Wisconsin. Individual research laboratories or institutes represented important agencies for research in California, New Mexico, and North Carolina. Finally, research in business administration and industrial and labor relations accounted for significant expenditures in the state universities of New Mexico and New York.

The University's Role in the State Scientific Effort

State universities in the six states have developed over the years highly important functions that they perform in connection with the scientific effort of their state governments. First, they bear major responsibility for basic research. California, for example, has an explicit policy that basic research shall be performed by the state university, and as a consequence regular state agencies are discouraged from undertaking basic investigations. In other states a similar practice has developed without any explicit statement of policy so that scientists on the staff of a state agency will refer to their professional colleagues at the state university questions arising in their applied research that merit further exploration of a more fundamental character.

The state universities also fulfill a role as applied research agencies. Their technical and professional schools, their research institutes and experiment stations, maintain close contact with organized groups in the state whose problems and needs provide some of the guidelines for planning applied research programs. Thus medical societies, state health departments, and research scientists on state university medical faculties are often in regular consultation. Farm groups make their needs known to experiment station scientists; highway departments and motor vehicle bureaus maintain consulting relationships with research engineers at the state college of engineering. Some of these associations are contractual and involve transfers of funds; others are very informal and any research involved is financed out of regular academic budgets. Here the state university is providing a highly important applied research service, sometimes focused upon problems of a state agency in its regulatory operations and at other times upon the needs and problems of some group of the state's citizens.

These two research functions, then, are part of the state university's mission as an agency of state government: (1) to conduct basic research; and (2) to carry on applied studies directed towards the needs of the state, its peoples, its governmental programs. In fulfilling the role expressed in these functions the state university is also furthering its fundamental objectives of training youth and advancing knowledge.

IV

Scientific Program Administration

CHAPTERS II AND III have presented a quantitative review of the scientific programs in six states. Expenditures for scientific activity, sources of funds, and professional manpower investment have been compared. Turning attention to how these scientific programs are administered, this chapter will discuss policies governing research, organizations engaging in scientific activity, efforts at program development and coordination, and the dissemination of the results of research. The study has not attempted to measure these aspects of program administration systematically, if indeed such phenomena can be so measured. Furthermore, systematic comparison of the states is difficult because the information available on program administration is uneven in the individual state reports. This discussion, then, is based upon qualitative, rather than quantitative, data.

SCIENTIFIC PROGRAMS AS AN ACTIVITY OF STATE GOVERNMENT

Members of the research staff engaged in this study were unanimous in their conclusion that in the six states, and probably in other states as well, research and related scientific activities are not considered a separate function of state government. Rather, state officials and researchers alike look upon scientific programs as instruments available to state government to use in the performance of its usual activities. Thus research is perceived as a tool the state employs to work towards such objectives as a more prosperous agricultural economy, a more efficient utilization of water resources, a more adequate control over the spread of infectious diseases, a more beautiful, safer, and better designed system of highways. This concept of scientific activities has been illustrated in many different ways in the supporting studies of individual states. Perhaps the best evidence is found in the heavy emphasis upon applied research and data collection in the programs of the majority of state agencies in every area of state activity except higher education.[1] Additional evidence lies in the kinds of research projects undertaken by various agencies in the six states as described in the state reports.

The organization of state agencies conducting scientific programs and the way budget and accounting systems record and report expenditures for such programs further reflect the assumption that the primary role of scientific activities is to serve operations. Relatively few agencies outside the universities and their affiliated agricultural and engineering experiment stations can be properly classed as line research organizations—that is, those in which a substantive program of research is the major focus and objective of the agency. Usually research units are established within operating agencies, or research responsibilities are assigned to regular operating divisions. The research performed is calculated to find answers to operating problems and to provide the bases for planning better programs.[2]

1. See the comparative analysis of expenditures for scientific activity during fiscal year 1954, Chapter II above, pp. 27-40.

2. Aside from the agricultural experiment stations and the state universities, state agencies wholly devoted to scientific activities and thus properly considered line research agencies tended to be located in the area of resource development and public works. Every state except Wisconsin reported such agencies: in California the Division of Mines in the Department of Natural Resources; in Connecticut the Geological and Natural History Survey; in New Mexico the Institute of Mining and Technology; in New York the Museum and Science Service in the Department of Education; and in North Carolina the Minerals Research Laboratory and Institute of Fisheries Research. New York's two health research institutes, Roswell Park Memorial Institute and the Psychiatric Institute, are also considered line research organizations.

Except in the case of agencies whose total budget is devoted to scientific activities, accounting systems in the states do not require a separate breakdown on research, and costs of scientific activities are accumulated in the same way costs of any other aspect of operating programs are recorded. Thus the significant figures needed to review and compare scientific programs across departmental lines cannot be readily obtained.

Because scientific activities are not considered a separate function of the government, policy makers in the executive branch and the legislature of the states examined do not express the concept of a comprehensive state scientific effort. Although many different kinds of governmental problems have been studied in the six states during recent years, none of these state governments has given thought to a study of the place of research in the state. Questions of the kinds raised in Chapter III concerning balance in the distribution of funds for scientific research among the various fields of government activity are not likely to be raised as long as awareness of scientific activities as a comprehensive program is lacking. Nor are these states likely to consider deliberately and systematically how much should be invested in research, for what purposes, and by what agencies and instruments of state government.

If such questions are not raised at the top policy-making level, is any consideration given to them? Is there any such thing as considered policy governing scientific programs as an activity of state government? The answer is that these issues are raised, if at all, at the departmental level, and they are likely to be raised in terms of alternative ways to meet operational needs. Developing policy on scientific activities at the departmental level tends to reinforce the concept that research is one of the available means to pursue an operating program.

POLICIES GOVERNING SCIENTIFIC ACTIVITIES

Although the study staff did not discover in any of the six states an elaborate, well developed body of official policies governing research—a code for the conduct of scientific activities—it is not true that the staff found nothing resembling policy concerning these programs. Marshall, for example, reports concerning California:

> Although the Legislature, the Governor and budget officials of the Department of Finance do not view the state as supporting an integrated research program, they have over the years elaborated a well-articulated set of policies to guide them in making decisions on the conduct of research; and these policies have been observed so closely that in more than one hundred interviews with department heads and research supervisors not a single official was discovered who was unaware of them.[3]

Formal policies on scientific activities in the six states tended to be of two kinds: (1) statements in statutes or administrative orders authorizing a particular agency to carry on research and data collection as one of the means to accomplish normal service or regulatory objectives; and (2) statements concerning the role of the university in research and the division of labor in scientific work between the university (including the agricultural experiment station) and the regular departments and agencies of state government.

The typical statutory authorization for scientific activity is a clear manifestation of the basic state policy regarding research and related work:[4] that it be practical and related

---

3. Marshall, California Report, Ch. 9.

4. An example is the following reference to the powers and duties of the Wisconsin Industrial Commission: "The commission . . . shall take all appropriate steps within its means to reduce and prevent unemployment. To this end the commission may employ experts and may carry on and publish the results of any investigations and research which it deems relevant. . . ." *Wisconsin Statutes*, 1953, 108.14 (6), quoted in Penniman, Wisconsin Report, Ch. 5. Rather than calling this statement scientific activity policy it would be more accurate to describe it as Wisconsin policy on preventing unemployment with authorization for scientific activities a by-product. Much policy governing the conduct of scientific activities is

to the attainment of a primary function of state government. This concept of research can be considered the fundamental policy underlying the entire structure of scientific activities in state government.

Another, less formal kind of policy on scientific work grows by implication from decisions to allocate funds to this agency or that to carry out some particular program of research. Such implied policies are undoubtedly conscious and deliberate on some occasions, but it is probably equally true that at other times the policy implications are neither conscious nor intended. When New York's governor approaches a particular man with a known interest in research to bring in as health commissioner, or when at the insistence of either the governor or his budget staff the New York Department of Mental Hygiene establishes the position of assistant commissioner for research and training, it can be fairly inferred that New York state government is pursuing a policy of major emphasis upon research in its health and mental health programs.[5] Without hesitation it can be said that each of the six states has a firm policy to support agricultural research related to the needs of the state's farmers. New Mexico and California with their pattern of expenditures for scientific activity demonstrate clear policy to stress research in the area of water resources. In many ways the examina-

in the same way an incidental part of a statement of state policy on some primary function.

5. Birkhead and Ahlberg, New York Report, Ch. 3. An incident in California illustrates the risk in inferring policy from actions that may be in response to political pressures rather than to actual policy decisions. Marshall reports that the California legislature for some years refused to follow the recommendation of the director of the Corrections Department to appropriate funds for a study of sex deviation. When public clamor built up over the sensational sex-murders of two small children in 1948, the legislature reversed itself and voted the funds to support the study. Marshall reports the outcome: "However, constant pressure from legislative committees for immediate results and budget cuts in ensuing years so disrupted the project that it died a slow death." California Report, Ch. 6. In this situation the state's policy concerning such research is hardly clear.

tion of expenditure patterns is a safer guide to policies than the scrutiny of legislative enactments and executive orders. Those policies concerned with the role of the state university in scientific activities and the division of labor between the university and the regular agencies of state governments, especially in regard to research, merit brief consideration. At least two of the states (California and Wisconsin) have explicit policies. California has for years firmly maintained that basic research financed from state funds shall be performed by the University of California. There has been no intent to de-emphasize basic research, for the legislature has supported such scientific work in the University of California handsomely in comparison to other states. Just as positively and firmly the operating agencies of state government are encouraged to carry on applied and developmental research programs.[6]

Wisconsin's approach has been somewhat different. In that state the policy is regularly stated and restated in legislative documents: "While some limited research by other state agencies is being done, the University should continue to be considered by the Legislature as the chief research arm of the state."[7] Furthermore, the Wisconsin policy is regularly reinforced by locating certain state scientific facilities on the campus of the University of Wisconsin in Madison. As of 1954 the state geologist was housed on the campus, and

6. Marshall, California Report, Ch. 9. It is interesting to note that the policy is almost fully effective, as measured by the analysis of expenditures for research in fiscal 1954 (see above, p. 31). In that year the University of California, including the agricultural experiment station, accounted for 99 per cent of the total expenditures for basic research made by state agencies. North Carolina and Wisconsin both reported 100 per cent of basic research expenditures accounted for by the state universities and agricultural experiment stations. These two states have not adopted an explicit policy of restricting state agencies from engaging in basic research and reserving this work for the universities. Actually, in these two states such a practice has developed without explicit policy.

7. Wisconsin Legislative Council, University of Wisconsin Policies, 1955 Committee Report, Vol. I, p. 6, quoted in Penniman, Wisconsin Report, Ch. 8.

his salary was part of the university budget. Both the Highway Materials Testing Laboratory and the State Laboratory of Hygiene were located in their own buildings constructed on the campus. During 1954 a new diagnostic center for mental health problems was opened on the campus under joint sponsorship and direction of the Department of Public Welfare and the University of Wisconsin.[8]

In North Carolina the university enjoys a traditional working relation with state government agencies much like that existing in Wisconsin. The university's role is not spelled out in written policy, nor is it articulated as conscious though unwritten policy. Nevertheless, for many kinds of problems arising in the course of regular state government operations, officials turn to university faculty members for consultation, advice, and in some cases actual research in seeking answers to operational problems.

Another important indicator of state policies concerning scientific work is the pattern of organization of scientific programs and the location of these organizations in state administrative structure.

TYPES OF ORGANIZATIONS ADMINISTERING SCIENTIFIC
PROGRAMS

The six states employ a wide variety of organizational structures to conduct research and related scientific activities. Even within a single state it is difficult to generalize about the different methods of organizing to carry on these programs.[9] Nevertheless, certain common types of organiza-

8. *Ibid.*, Ch. 8. Birkhead and Ahlberg, New York Report, Ch. 10, have a good discussion of the points advanced on both sides of the question of assigning full responsibility for basic research to the state university. In a state like New York, where regular state agencies are already engaged in carrying on important basic research programs, there is a serious question whether allocation of full responsibility for such work to universities would be desirable or even feasible.

9. For example, Lehmann, Connecticut Report, Ch. 9; Marshall, California Report, Ch. 9; Birkhead and Ahlberg, New York Report, Ch. 3; and Penniman, Wisconsin Report, Ch. 9.

tional form and program purpose or objective run through the differences.

Agencies carrying on scientific activities in the six states can be classified into three types on the basis of their major purpose or objective. One group consists of those organizations pursuing scientific work as their main program objective—the scientific program agencies such as the agricultural experiment stations, New York's Psychiatric Institute, New Mexico's Institute of Mining and Technology, California's Division of Mines, or North Carolina's Institute of Fisheries Research. The various state universities also fit into this category. The second type is made up of organizations carrying on research and gathering data as a direct aid to operations. These operations-related scientific agencies would include such organizations as the research units in fish and game departments, forestry and water resource divisions, highway department research laboratories, statistical divisions in departments of banking and insurance, and research units in various health departments engaged in problem-solving studies. Third, there are in every state certain staff scientific agencies carrying on scientific work as an aid to department management in program planning, review, and evaluation. This group includes such organizations as the division of research and statistics in state departments of public welfare, education, employment security, and in some cases public health and agriculture. Clearly, these categories are not mutually exclusive. At times a scientific program agency, for example an agricultural experiment station, may conduct studies directly focused upon operating problems referred to the station by the state agriculture department. In this case the station is functioning as an operations-related agency.

Scientific program agencies tend to be independent establishments, or if within a department, they are likely to be largely autonomous. In contrast, the operations-related agencies tend to be located in departments with major operating responsibilities. Scientific program agencies look to research scientists for their top leadership and major staff. Research is normally conducted on a project basis, and individual researchers enjoy considerable freedom in the selection of projects, the development of research plans, and the conduct of research. Researchers are generally protected from pressures associated with operating agencies. They are afforded wider opportunities to attend professional meetings and confer with professional colleagues, and they are given encouragement or even required to write for the scientific journals.

Some, but not all, scientific program agencies place major emphasis upon basic research; indeed, very little basic research is carried on in any of the six states except in such agencies. Furthermore, certain of them have a clearly defined clientele directly interested in the results of their research. In such cases these organizations can be said to provide a research service. The agricultural experiment stations fit this description, as do North Carolina's Institute of Fisheries Research and the various minerals-research agencies. Their emphasis is upon applied research and in some cases development.

The operations-related group probably represents the largest number of organizations engaged in scientific activities in the six states, although clearly the scientific program agencies (including both universities and agricultural experiment stations) account for a larger proportion of total expenditures for scientific activities. The operations-related group includes the isolated individual in a regular operating division who devotes part of his time to operations and part to careful and systematic trouble-shooting studies, as well as the separate research bureau set up by a department to conduct studies on those operating problems identified by line division heads as requiring immediate study. Program decisions on research and data-collection activities in such organizations are likely to be made by higher authority rather than by the researchers themselves. Although publication of results may be encouraged in some or even most such agencies, a considerable part of their scientific work does not lend itself to dissemination beyond the operating departments.

Staff scientific agencies are most likely to stress social science techniques and the gathering of data on social phenomena.[10] Usually these units are located near the departmental executive, in some cases reporting directly to him. These researchers are not primarily interested in specific problems of operations and their detailed solutions; instead, their role is to collect the kinds of data and develop the analytical tools necessary for critical program review, identification of gaps and imbalance requiring program development, and measurement of efficiency and effectiveness in existing programs. Such research staffs can often supply top management with much of the analysis leading to basic program decisions. Of the three classes of organizations, staff agencies are the fewest in number and the least well developed, and certainly their activities absorb a much smaller share of both expenditures and manpower investment in scientific activities.

Important variables differentiating organizations in the six states are the size and complexity of structure. For example, North Carolina and New Mexico have very few governmental organizations in which research is the sole or even primary objective; furthermore, much of the operations-related research is actually performed on the side by individuals in fulltime operating positions. State departments in

10. The following are examples of some of the staff scientific agencies identified in the state reports: in New York the Health Department Office of Program Development and Evaluation and the Education Department Office of Research and Special Studies (Birkhead and Ahlberg, New York Report, Ch. 7); in California the Research and Statistics Section of the Department of Employment (Marshall, California Report, Ch. 5); and in North Carolina the Public Welfare Department Research and Statistical Service (Cleaveland and Johns, North Carolina Report, Ch. 6).

New York or California for the most part will organize research units whose major purpose is to conduct the troubleshooting studies often carried on in New Mexico and North Carolina by individual operating officials. New York has developed more highly specialized and differentiated organization for conducting scientific activities than any state under examination. Fifteen of the eighteen executive departments in New York state government reported permanent agencies at bureau or division level with scientific activities as their major responsibility. In three of these departments an assistant commissioner has the principal duty of research supervision throughout the department.[11] At the other extreme, Richards and Radosevich reported that "internal organization for the purpose of scientific activity is at a minimum in New Mexico, even in administrative units where research constitutes the main purpose."[12]

One final aspect of research organization bears brief examination in this discussion, namely, the organizational aspects of financing scientific activities. In several of the states, notably New Mexico, Wisconsin, and North Carolina, a number of departments engaging in research and related activities are financed out of earmarked revenues received by the state. Typically, these are agencies serving an identifiable clientele capable of shouldering the burdens of a special tax. Thus the fish and game departments draw their financial support from the receipts of hunting and fishing licenses, sale of publications, and other miscellaneous sources. Highway departments are financed out of a special highway fund dependent primarily upon gasoline taxes for its income. The existence of these special financial arrangements modify the status of the agency, curtailing the influence of the governor and his budget staff over agency program and budget. Of course, the department must still come to the legislature for

11. Birkhead and Ahlberg, New York Report, Ch. 3.
12. Richards and Radosevich, New Mexico Report, Ch. 4.

appropriation out of the segregated fund; nevertheless, since the money requested does not come out of general state funds but out of an earmarked source, the legislature and governor are more likely to pass over proposals lightly and to approve them without careful scrutiny. Such is decidedly not the case with program proposals to be financed out of general funds. As noted in Chapter I, a related consequence of these earmarked funds is to splinter the governor's authority over the executive departments of state government. From the point of view of the agency there are some distinct advantages in special financing out of segregated funds. Research proposals contained in the budget of an agency financed out of an earmarked fund would probably not be cut out by the governor or legislature on grounds of inadequate revenues.[13] A somewhat similar, though not identical, situation is presented by those few agencies financed directly out of assessments levied against their organized clientele. Organizations such as the various industry advisory committees active in the agricultural area in California, or the Oil and Gas Division of California's Department of Natural Resources, fit this description. The Oil and Gas Division, for example, is financed by charges levied against the oil and gas industry in the state. Much of its data-gathering work facilitates the growth and prosperity of the industry. An agency financed either under this arrangement or by a segregated fund derived from its most interested clientele is likely to be unusually sensitive to the interests and desires of those special pleaders.

Perhaps the experience of certain state universities in financing research through private nonprofit foundations has some application to regular state operations. Of particular interest in this connection is the Wisconsin Alumni Research Fund, a local foundation established at the university to assist

13. Penniman, Wisconsin Report, Ch. 4, contains a discussion of the special funds for the Department of Conservation and the Highway Commission.

in encouraging and financing faculty research, especially in the life and physical sciences. The Fund was originally established with income derived from patents developed by a faculty member at the University of Wisconsin; it has grown steadily through wise investment and assignment of additional patents to the Fund from time to time.[14] State University of New York has recently established a research foundation to serve as "trustee and administrator of gifts and grants in aid" and, through contractual agreements with State University, to undertake "to conduct many research programs financed by funds supplied from sources other than appropriations of the state legislature."[15] Other universities among those examined have employed similar devices to receive gifts and grants and to administer them in support of research.

PROGRAM FORMULATION AND COORDINATION

A discussion of program administration is incomplete without a consideration of the program planning process through which organizations seek to develop and carry out their scientific activity. In many ways this process of program formulation and coordination is the heart of program administration. Program planning has developed as an essential tool in administrative management to provide the whole organization with a sense of direction and to insure that results of the work carried out by various segments of the organization will be cumulative in their contribution to the basic objective of the agency. Departments engaged in scientific activity, whether they be scientific program agencies or operating departments employing research and data collection as a tool to accomplish operating ends, need the sense of cohesion and direction that comes from both the process

14. *Ibid.*, Ch. 8.
15. The Research Foundation of State University of New York, *2nd Annual Report* (Albany: The Foundation, 1953), p. 7, as quoted in Birkhead and Ahlberg, New York Report, Ch. 9.

of program formulation and the product, or program, the process yields.

This study revealed that although the awareness of scientific programs was greater at the level of the department head than in the governor's office and legislative halls, there were nevertheless many agencies engaging in scientific endeavor where these activities were no more than a collection of unrelated units of work. Perhaps they had been initiated in response to some need expressed by an operating official, a field officer, a member of the clientele served by the agency. Seldom were these scientific activities of the agency systematically and regularly scrutinized to determine wherein they were related, how they might be combined or recombined more efficiently, or whether activities begun long ago should be abandoned for more important work. Still less frequent were the occasions when agencies engaged in closely related operating programs consulted together on how their scientific activities might be better coordinated. Also, as already indicated, in no state was there clear evidence of progress towards the development of government-wide program development in the area of research and related activities. The following discussion will focus attention on the fragmentary evidence reflecting a conscious process of program planning at whatever level.

Program Development at the Departmental Level

In all six states the process of program formulation was found to be more highly developed in the scientific program agencies, particularly the agricultural experiment stations. At each station the research program is developed through a systematic and continuing process generally similar and including at least the following steps: initiation of a project proposal by the researcher; critical review by a group of professional colleagues; and approval or rejection of the project. In addition each active project is reviewed periodically and progress towards completion is recorded. To guide this initiation and approval process the station develops sets of priorities ranking subject-matter areas and specific research problems in terms of importance to the state's agricultural economy. From time to time representatives of various farm groups may be invited to participate in experiment station conferences to work out these priorities. The accumulated group of active projects plus those proposed for future work constitutes the core of the station's budget request before the state legislature.[16]

In some cases operations-related agencies and staff scientific groups use a system generally similar to that described above in the development of their research programs.[17] It is probably true, however, that the process of proposal, review, and approval is somewhat more formal and systematically followed in the agricultural experiment stations than elsewhere outside the universities. The Wisconsin Department of Conservation has established a Research Advisory Committee of three professional men from outside the agency and a Steering Committee of selected representatives from operating divisions to join in regular review of the Department's research program plans and to assist in setting priorities and guiding future program development.[18] North Carolina's commissioner of public welfare uses an *ad hoc* committee of agency staff to work out research designs for a project and then converts a full staff meeting of headquarters and field representatives into a project-reviewing committee to evaluate and refine proposed projects.[19]

16. Marshall, California Report, Ch. 3; Richards and Radosevich, New Mexico Report, Ch. 4; Birkhead and Ahlberg, New York Report, Ch. 4; Cleaveland and Johns, North Carolina Report, Ch. 3; and Penniman, Wisconsin Report, Ch. 3.

17. Penniman, Wisconsin Report, Ch. 4 and Ch. 6, discusses the Departments of Conservation and Public Welfare.

18. *Ibid.*, Ch. 4.

19. Cleaveland and Johns, North Carolina Report, Ch. 6.

Not all agencies engaged in scientific activities organize their research and data-gathering efforts around identifiable projects. Instead of specific, individual studies the work may require repetitive activities such as continuing collection and analysis of certain kinds of data. Perhaps the main effort is to perform a trouble-shooting function whenever difficulties arise in an operating program. In these situations the program planning process is likely to be more informal, initiative resting with the head of the research staff rather than with individual researchers as in the case of the program built up of separate projects. As Lehmann observes in the Connecticut Report:

In the case of applied and development research carried on as an incidental part of operating activities, research is likely to be of the "trouble-shooting" variety which scarcely lends itself to careful advance planning. The separately organized research units, however, do normally carry on their activities within the framework of a planned research program. Generally the director of such a research unit carries on the actual program planning, often in consultation with an agency commissioner and his administrative assistants and perhaps also conferring with chiefs of operational units most directly concerned.[20]

In all six states the budget review process provides a means for central control over scientific activity and at the same time an opportunity for program evaluation, planning, and decision making at the departmental level. This process may not be quite so important in the agricultural experiment stations with their well developed system of project initiation and approval, but particularly for the operations-related and the staff scientific agencies this budget review in many cases provides the only real opportunity for examination of agency-wide program. Marshall observes that in California those operating agencies that have dispersed scientific activities widely to many subdivisions make little distinc-

20. Lehmann, Connecticut Report, Ch. 9.

tion in budget review between scientific and operating programs. By contrast, he finds that in departments where scientific activities tend to be concentrated in a few subdivisions, research programs are much more likely to receive direct and special attention apart from operations.[21] In Wisconsin, too, virtually all planning or program review takes place through the budget process. Yet typically the budget does not provide a separate breakdown of the estimates of costs for research and related scientific activity; instead these items are lumped in with the general estimates.[22]

New York and California appear to have been most imaginative in trying to develop the kind of institutions around the department head to make possible effective departmental program planning in the area of scientific activities.[23] In both states health and mental health organizations have made good progress in this direction. The Office of Program Development and Evaluation established by New York's Health Department is worth noting in particular. This office, headed by an assistant commissioner, has department-wide responsibility for encouraging operating divisions to develop better methods of program self-evaluation and of estimating public health needs in the state. It supervises, promotes, and conducts research and works to coordinate the various research committees and activities scattered throughout the New York Health Department. By establishing this staff scientific agency, the Department has clearly demonstrated "its understanding of the central role of research in program development and evaluation."[24] The

21. Marshall, California Report, Ch. 9. An interesting procedure is followed in California's Department of Public Health, where a reviewing committee composed of the director and his six division chiefs conducts an annual program review supplementing the budget review. This annual review emphasizes program accomplishments and plans rather than fiscal matters. Ibid., Ch. 9.

22. Penniman, Wisconsin Report, Ch. 9.

23. Birkhead and Ahlberg, New York Report, Ch. 3.

24. Ibid., Ch. 7.

organization of New York's Department of Mental Hygiene also reflects the policy of top-management responsibility for directing scientific activities. The Department has established an assistant commissioner for research and training who exercises broad supervisory responsibility for research throughout the Department. Spending more than half his time at field establishments, this assistant commissioner provides the coordinating influence otherwise lacking in this agency.[25]

California's departments and agencies engaged in scientific activities almost all rely on some form of committee review, staff meeting, or conference to evaluate programs and reach decisions on future plans.[26] The agencies in the general area of mental health and corrections have gone further and involved private citizens, citizen organizations, and outside professional groups in the committee review. As Marshall suggests, since the mental health and correction agencies are "research-minded" but in 1954 had not yet succeeded in winning continued public and legislative support, these advisory committees may well serve a promotional function as well as the purpose of program development and coordination. This well developed committee system is perhaps best illustrated by reference to the Research Standing Committee of the Department of Mental Hygiene. Staffed by outstanding state officials in the mental health field, the Committee in 1954 was undertaking to develop a comprehensive research program for the Department, focusing particular attention upon the establishment of research priorities.[27]

Interdepartmental Program Coordination

In addition to the efforts described above to develop both institutions and procedures for program planning at the departmental level, some of the states have experimented with interdepartmental coordination of related scientific programs.

25. *Ibid.*, Ch. 7.
26. Marshall, California Report, Ch. 9.
27. *Ibid.*, Ch. 6.

Wisconsin, for example, created the Natural Resources Committee of State Agencies in 1951 to coordinate the activities (including research) of several state agencies active in resource development. The Committee, with no direct appropriation and no staff of its own, works through a system of subcommittees, with participating agencies providing personnel and in some cases needed services. Probably its most important contribution has been to provide a forum for exchange of ideas and a collaborative experience to encourage conservation agencies to work together more regularly.[28]

Among the six states under study California has made by far the most extensive use of interdepartmental committees, and with some success. These committees in general have been composed of representatives from departments and agencies with related research interests. The committee structure has afforded them opportunity to exchange ideas on their scientific work, review technical questions, and work out problems of research design and methodology. Without formal authority and with no function but to advise, these groups have been able to bring informed professional opinion to bear upon research problems. They have helped to eliminate duplication by coordinating research efforts; they have worked out clear lines of division of research labor among several agencies; they have engaged in joint planning of research and, in at least one case, have actually conducted research. They have worked out standards for classification of data and established priorities to guide development of research programs; they have even gone out to seek foundation support for worthy research that could not be financed out of state appropriations. Perhaps the most important and certainly one of the most successful interagency bodies has been the Interdepartmental Research Coordinating Committee made up chiefly of representatives from agencies engaged in socio-economic research. This committee has con-

28. Penniman, Wisconsin Report, Ch. 4.

centrated its attention particularly upon coordinating and trying to improve programs of data collection and analysis. In Marshall's words, the Committee "has eliminated duplication of effort and measurably strengthened the quality of statistical research and reporting in many state agencies. And it has served, also, as a means of coordinating research efforts on problems which spill across departmental lines."[29]

Interstate and Federal Influence on Program Coordination

The state reports identify a number of different points at which federal agencies and interstate instrumentalities have contributed to more effective program coordination and program development. This influence of the federal agencies stems at least in part from their role as grantors of important funds used to finance scientific activity. In addition federal scientists and their colleagues at the state level in general maintain an association marked by mutual professional confidence and respect. In this situation federal scientists would in all probability have considerable influence over program developments in the state agency whether a grant-in-aid arrangement existed or not.

Such federal agencies as the Department of Agriculture, the Fish and Wildlife Service, the Bureau of Public Roads, and the Public Health Service have an important role in the planning and coordination of certain research undertakings in particular states. The Department of Agriculture, for example, may be given responsibility by Congress to coordinate the development of a cooperative research program through the experiment stations, focusing on some particular

29. Marshall, California Report, Ch. 9. New York employs a similar device, the Interdepartmental Committee on Economic Research, to help coordinate economic research and accompanying statistical analysis carried on by state agencies. New York also uses the interdepartmental committee made up of department heads, like the Mental Health Commission and the Youth Commission, to concentrate attention and state resources upon a particular problem. Such interdepartmental agencies sometimes engage in research themselves. Birkhead and Ahlberg, New York Report, Ch. 3 and Ch. 7.

agricultural problem which is regional in scope. The Department of Agriculture then participates with the experiment station members in planning the research and working out the division of labor necessary.[30]

Another case of federal participation in state agency program development is the United States Public Health Service requirement of advance program plans. In order to qualify for certain kinds of grants from the Public Health Service the particular state health agency must prepare a formal and detailed program plan covering a specified period of years. In those state health departments where there has been no earlier tradition of program planning, this federal requirement has had the effect of stimulating establishment of at least the rudiments of program planning.

Another organization which has contributed towards better research planning and coordination at the state level is the National Highway Research Board. This board, established as a part of the National Research Council, serves as a kind of clearinghouse for state highway departments, the Bureau of Public Roads, and professional engineering research groups. In 1945 the Board inaugurated the Research Correlation Service to help keep interested agencies, both public and private, informed about current developments in highway research throughout the country. The Service has helped state highway departments avoid costly duplication of research already underway or completed elsewhere; it has also facilitated the Board's efforts to bring groups of state highway agencies together in cooperative research. Conceivably the states through the Council of State Governments might consider the establishment of similar interstate clearinghouse agencies in other fields where considerable research is underway. Some federal agencies, like the Office of Ex-

30. *Ibid.*, Ch. 4, contains a statement by the director of the Cornell experiment station concerning the importance of cooperative regional research projects and the role of the United States Department of Agriculture in the administration of these projects.

periment Stations, United States Department of Agriculture, and the Fish and Wildlife Service, already serve this interstate coordination function and provide the means for exchange of information among state research agencies in their particular fields.

Professional associations of state government officials also perform a coordinating role. By meeting together from time to time and discussing operations and research these groups provide opportunity for coordination. Some associations actually engage in occasional research and data collection.[31] Although such professional societies are most important in developing the sense of professionalism among some of these specialized officials in state government, they are probably not well equipped to handle the major responsibilities for a systematic effort at research coordination. It would appear more appropriate to rely upon them for supplemental assistance in the form of an informal clearinghouse for scientific activities through annual meetings.

DISSEMINATING THE RESULTS OF SCIENTIFIC ACTIVITIES

A final and important aspect of administering scientific work is the communication of the results of research and data collection to those who can make use of them. The job of communication can become exceedingly complex when the objective is to make particular research results available to many different audiences, including the lay public as well as the scientific public. In this situation the job calls for interpretation of the scientific results and translation into concepts and symbols suited to the various audiences to be reached. Although this study of state government scientific activities gave attention to scientific information and its dissemination as one of the components of scientific activity, the data gathered on this component were generally disappointing. Identifiable expenditures for this purpose were quite

31. The National Association of Rail and Utility Commissioners is a good example. Penniman, Wisconsin Report, Ch. 5.

modest and did not reflect the emphasis placed upon disseminating research results in most of the states. In many cases where a report was issued describing a particular piece of research, the costs attached to this publication could not be separated out and as a result were reported as part of the research expenditure. In other cases dissemination to scientific audiences was accomplished through publication in a professional journal where no expenditure was involved, and the time invested was reported as time devoted to the conduct of research. As far as this component of scientific activity is concerned, dollars expended proved to be a completely inadequate measure.

Despite the incomplete data collected on the dissemination of scientific information, a few general observations can be made. The agricultural experiment stations appear to have progressed further than other agencies covered by the study in systematically developing techniques for disseminating information. All the stations have their own publication program aimed at the primary consumer of their research service—the farmer. The facilities of the agricultural extension service are available to scientists in the experiment station for interpreting and reporting their research to farmers through demonstration meetings, through special publications, through radio and television broadcasts, through local farm papers—in short, through every one of the mass media. For the scientific audiences, the experiment stations may publish either in their own technical journal and pamphlet series or in professional journals in fields related to agriculture.[32]

In general the same techniques were used to disseminate information by the same groups of agencies in each state. A number of state departments carry on their own publication

32. Penniman, Wisconsin Report, Ch. 3; Birkhead and Ahlberg, New York Report, Ch. 4; Lehmann, Connecticut Report, Ch. 3; and Marshall, California Report, Ch. 3.

program. New York state government, for example, finances the publication of at least six scientific journals; only one of these is in the field of agriculture. Most of the scientific program agencies encourage their staff members to submit manuscripts to professional journals regularly; indeed in some of these agencies promotion may be based in part upon the publication record of the individual. Scientific conferences and professional society meetings afford state agencies still another means of communicating the results of research to technical and professional audiences.

In the program areas, where federal departments participate through grants-in-aid and where regular consultation on programs takes place between state and federal personnel, provision is frequently made for federal or joint federal-state publication of research. The *Pittman-Robertson Quarterly* and *Dingell-Johnson Quarterly* published by the United States Fish and Wildlife Service are examples. The pages of these two quarterly journals are devoted largely to reporting research underway and completed in state departments of fish and game financed through the Pittman-Robertson and Dingell-Johnson federal grant funds. Frequently, ground-water and surface-water analyses and studies carried on cooperatively by the United States Geological Survey and a state division of water resources are published in the regular monograph series of the Survey; at other times such cooperative studies may be published as parts in a series of state publications on water resources.

All these methods are available and all of them are used to good advantage by state government departments engaged in scientific activities. However, the individual state reports suggest that, despite these efforts and the many alternative media of communication, there is still significant scientific work not adequately reported. The writers of the New York Report conclude regarding this matter of communicating the results of scientific activities: "Here is a problem deserving the attention of state officials, federal officials, private foundations, and professional groups. More media for communication of research results could contribute importantly to improved governmental performance in these areas."[33]

33. Birkhead and Ahlberg, New York Report, Ch. 10.

V

Intergovernmental Relations

IN THE BRIEF GLIMPSE of the American federal system in Chapter I, it was quite apparent that the relations between the states and the federal government have been significantly modified by the expansion in both the scope and volume of governmental activity at all levels. The expanding role of government, built in part upon cooperation and collaboration between the states and the central government, marks a clear departure from nineteenth-century notions of federalism based upon the restrictive concept of exclusive spheres of activity for each level of government. The changing ideas about the nature of the union and the newly developing relations between the states and the federal government have come partly as a response to the demands of citizens for more aggressive governmental efforts to resolve the many new kinds of problems raised by modern urban-industrial society. As John Gaus has expressed it: "No problem of any consequence which affects our local communities or national strength can be solved, or seriously attacked, in this country unless the resources of every level of government operating in a given area are mobilized to supplement (not supplant) each other."[1]

The same problems characteristic of the twentieth century have also created the need for increasing emphasis upon scientific work as an activity of government. The states as well as the national government are depending more and more upon scientific research for aid in meeting the demands

1. J. M. Gaus, *Reflections on Public Administration* (University, Alabama: University of Alabama Press, 1947), p. 80.

of their citizens for services and facilities considered essential to modern life.

Against the background of cooperative federalism and an expanding role for scientific research as a governmental activity, what light does this study shed on intergovernmental relations? More specifically, what kinds of relationships exist between states and the federal government and between one state and another in the conduct of scientific activity? How have the relations of the states to the federal government and the states to each other affected these scientific programs? These questions are the concern of this chapter.

THE FEDERAL GOVERNMENT AND STATE SCIENTIFIC ACTIVITY

The fields of scientific research and development provide an excellent vehicle for studying federal-state relations in the United States, particularly because agencies at the two levels of government have worked out many different kinds of relationships in these scientific programs. In some cases the relations are informal and involve scientists who jointly share a field operation. At the other extreme, agencies may draw up a formal contract calling for joint financing of a project with responsibility for actual performance set forth in detail. There may be general grants for research in a broad area, or there may be specific grants tied to individual projects or to research on a carefully delimited subject. The state may or may not be required to match the federal grant. An almost infinite variety of combinations of these different features can be put together in any one program of scientific work.

Perhaps the simplest relation between state and federal agencies concerned with scientific activities is that organized around the exchange of information. In the field of natural resources and public works, for example, state and federal agencies with common interests in gathering basic physical data often work out a kind of informal division of labor, relying on one another for different segments of these data. Thus the Wisconsin Committee on Water Pollution works with similar organizations in several neighboring states and with a number of federal agencies, including the Geological Survey, the Fish and Wildlife Service, and the Public Health Service. All participating agencies are engaged in gathering information necessary to determine the degree of pollution in certain streams, the nature of the pollutants, and their effect on animal and human life.[2] This kind of exchange of information can take place without any transfer of funds or grant; alternatively, it can be part of a more elaborate relation involving transfer of funds, joint work in actual data collection, and joint analysis.

Another arrangement between state and federal agencies in pursuit of scientific work might be classified as cooperative studies. Again the individual state reports are full of illustrative examples in the area of resource development and public works. In most of the six states the United States Geological Survey and perhaps two or three state and other federal agencies carry on cooperative programs of research and data collection. In North Carolina, for example, the Water Resources Division of the Department of Conservation and Development and the Geological Survey have collaborated on studies of surface-water resources in the state and the chemical quality of water. The Division operates certain stream gauging stations; others are manned by the Geological Survey, by the Tennessee Valley Authority, and by the United States Army Corps of Engineers. Publication of results is handled jointly.[3]

State forestry divisions in California, New York, North Carolina, and Wisconsin cooperate with the United States Forest Service and the regional forest experiment stations in gathering various kinds of data and conducting research.

2. Penniman, Wisconsin Report, Ch. 4.
3. Cleaveland and Johns, North Carolina Report, Ch. 4.

In certain projects personnel from state and federal agencies may work side by side, some work parties supervised by federal foresters and others by state foresters. Equipment may be furnished by one or both agencies involved; there may be a pooling of funds to finance a particular project, or one or more parties may contribute personnel and equipment rather than funds. Sometimes actual formal contracts may be drawn up; or again the field staffs of two agencies may get together informally to work on a problem of common interest.

Illustrations of cooperative studies can also be drawn from several other areas of government activity. In agriculture the operation of the Joint Federal-State Crop and Livestock Reporting Service, for example, illustrates how close the working relationship can be between state and federal officials in a cooperative enterprise for gathering and disseminating data.[4] Another interesting relation exists between the United States Bureau of Labor Statistics and the California Division of Labor Statistics and Research. The federal bureau does not subsidize the state scientific work by a grant of funds; instead, the Bureau of Labor Statistics makes available to the state organization several of its professional staff to assist in collection and analysis of data in which the federal bureau is interested. These economists and statisticians are recruited from a federal civil service register and are paid by federal funds, but they work under direction of the California Division of Labor Statistics and Research.[5]

The granting of financial aid represents a third type of relation between state and federal agencies in scientific activities. The grants include any kind of money grant by a federal agency to finance scientific activity carried on by a state government agency. First, there are grant-in-aid programs to

---

4. Penniman, *Wisconsin Report*, Ch. 3; Birkhead and Ahlberg, *New York Report*, Ch. 4; Marshall, *California Report*, Ch. 3; and Cleaveland and Johns, *North Carolina Report*, Ch. 3.
5. Marshall, *California Report*, Ch. 5.

support research in the agricultural experiment stations, where the federal funds go to finance individual research projects that fit into the program specifications of federal legislation. Somewhat similar programs exist in the fish and wildlife areas where the Dingell-Johnson and Pittman-Robertson statutes authorize federal grants to support research and data-gathering activities that meet the substantive requirements of these laws. Administrative arrangements under such grants call for the research scientist in the state agency to propose projects and federal officials to review and pass on the qualifications of the projects for support.

Grants of the kinds made to employment security programs and the public assistance work of state departments of public welfare are less likely to be tied to specific projects. Instead, these grants are part of the general support program through which the federal government finances state administration of employment security and public welfare programs. From the supporting federal funds a portion goes to research and statistical units in state employment security agencies and departments of public welfare; these funds may be considered grants to finance scientific activity (largely the gathering and analysis of data on social phenomena).

Federal grants to support highway research are another kind of grant. Here the basic program provides that 1.5 per cent of total federal grants for highway purposes shall be used to finance highway research, as long as the state has matched these federal grant funds according to the prescribed formula. The basic legislation also requires a state to establish laboratory facilities for research in order to qualify for federal aid. This approach has stimulated considerable expansion of highway research in the states.

One other variation of the grant-in-aid program should be mentioned. Increasingly in recent years the United States Public Health Service and the National Institutes of Health have used categorical grants to support research. These federal agencies have tended to make grants for research on such diseases as heart disease, cancer, and mental health, rather than to grant general funds for medical research. The researcher employing funds granted for research on one of these diseases does not have full freedom to pursue basic investigations unless his studies are rather directly tied to the disease in question. Categorical grants are characteristic of federal health programs supporting research in non-federal agencies, including state university medical schools, hospitals, and medical research organizations like New York's Roswell Park Memorial Institute and the Psychiatric Institute. Conversely, proportionally fewer general grants have been made to such state health research agencies.[6]

Also in the area of health, education, and welfare another type of federal grant program has been used quite extensively as a means to support state scientific activities: aid for the training of scientific manpower. Federal agencies like the Public Health Service and the Children's Bureau, for example, provide funds to enable professional personnel in state medical institutions and welfare departments to obtain advanced scientific training. The programs vary considerably in detail from residency training arrangements to educational leaves and graduate fellowships awarded to enable the recipients to attend graduate school.[7]

The authors of the six state reports are in substantial agreement that federal grants have generally stimulated the growth of state scientific programs. In one way or another these grants have had a "pump-priming" effect. In California, for example, Marshall observes that because federal grants made to support scientific work in the Department of Employment and in the Health Department's Bureau of Chronic Diseases have relieved the state of the necessity to

6. Birkhead and Ahlberg, New York Report, Ch. 10.
7. For example, Penniman, Wisconsin Report, Ch. 6; Lehmann, Connecticut Report, Ch. 6; and Cleaveland and Johns, North Carolina Report, Ch. 6.

finance these programs, it is possible for California to use state funds for the expansion of scientific activity in other fields.[8]

New York agencies have found federal grants for research particularly helpful because of the added flexibility they bring. One department, for example, employs its federal money to finance new projects; then, once assured of their worth and feasibility, the department transfers them to state appropriations. In this way the agency finds it possible to do some experimenting and to expand its research program as the experiments prove successful. The authors of the New York Report also point out that federal grants "insure the presence of a minimum research staff" in an agency. Without at least this minimum qualified staff it might prove impossible to conduct scientific research. In some of the smaller states a federal grant in a given area may be the absolute prerequisite to maintaining any research staff at all.[9]

In other situations the federal grant may prove to be the only way to strengthen or expand state scientific work. At times when a state government is subject to particularly heavy pressures for economy, as Wisconsin was in 1954, an offer of federal funds may be the only stimulus strong enough to bring a legislature and an executive budget staff to provide further support for scientific research.[10]

There are other important considerations besides the pump-priming quality of federal grants for research. For example, what price does a state have to pay when it accepts this federal stimulant? Or to put it another way, in making grants to finance scientific activity does the federal agency tend to control or influence important state decisions about the allocation of scientific funds? Once the federal government offers grants-in-aid to finance research in a particular area, does the state really have any freedom of choice left?

8. Marshall, California Report, Ch. 9.
9. Birkhead and Ahlberg, New York Report, Ch. 10.
10. Penniman, Wisconsin Report, Ch. 10.

Implications in the New York, Connecticut, New Mexico, and Wisconsin reports hint that a narrowing of choices open to a state may occur.

The authors of the New York Report are quite explicit about the loss of state control over policy in those areas where federal agencies make categorical grants. "Categorical grants fail to take into account the special needs, facilities, staff and interests of the departments at the state level. They substitute congressional and federal executive policy for state policy."[11]

The Connecticut Report raises another kind of question about the possible tendency towards undue federal influence over state research policy. Commenting on attitudes expressed by state officials in Connecticut regarding federal grants, Lehmann writes:

Others made the pointed observation that certain research activities of the state were conducted largely because federal money was available. In other words, there is no longer a real need, for example, for research in tuberculosis, while such areas as old age and mental health urgently require expansion of research efforts to resolve their growing problems; yet these areas receive little or no federal aid. This would appear to be a valid criticism of some federal aid programs for lacking sufficient sensitivity and responsiveness to the changing needs of the states. Some federal agencies rather seem to support certain areas of activity because of tradition and established precedent, even after the need for the support has disappeared or become much less urgent than the need for support in other fields of research.[12]

11. Birkhead and Ahlberg, New York Report, Ch. 10.
12. Lehmann, Connecticut Report, Ch. 10. A somewhat different complaint was heard in California. There on several occasions a federal agency has withdrawn support from well established programs which were serving a real need and on which the state depended. In this situation some California agency has moved in to maintain the service. Marshall observes: "The problem is not a serious one, of course, but state agencies do resent picking up the check if the national government abandons a program when it may be approaching its most productive stages." California Report, Ch. 9.

Fears and resentments are also associated with irritations concerning the administrative controls some federal grantors maintain over the state agencies carrying on programs financed by them. The California and New York reports, in particular, note the complaints of state officials about complicated reporting and accounting requirements imposed by federal agencies. These irritations are probably inevitable in any arrangement necessitating two sets of accounts, one for the state and a second for the federal agency involved. Both state reports argue for the advantages to be gained through more flexibility in grant-in-aid administration. They suggest that a federal granting agency set high standards for accounting and reporting and exercise discretion, imposing uniform detailed requirements only on those states failing to meet the standards. Other states would not be required to follow uniform procedures as long as their systems measured up to the standards, even though any particular system might differ in detail from that recommended by the federal agency.[13]

Not all state opinion reported in this study was fearful of federal influence over state policy and programs exercised through grants-in-aid. Marshall finds that California has retained reasonably full control over scientific policy, because "in regard to most federally aided functions, the state more than meets the federal matching requirement, and accordingly it cannot be held that the desire to secure federal money is forcing the state to spend for functions it would prefer to ignore or support on a more modest basis."[14] Lehmann,

13. Marshall, California Report, Ch. 9. In the clear words of Birkhead and Ahlberg: "Here again, the goal should be to relax restrictions and to differentiate requirements in terms of the quality of state personnel and program. Uniform policy and procedures may be simple to administer but should not be confused with good administration." New York Report, Ch. 10.

14. Marshall, California Report, Ch. 9. He goes on in a similar vein to suggest that perhaps in some areas the federal grant procedure opens the way for state officials to influence federal policy strongly, rather than the reverse. He says: "And, indeed, any sophisticated analysis of the

in discussing the Connecticut situation, is also in general agreement with the position Marshall has taken. In his mind federal financial aid has not been the only, or even the dominant, stimulus to the initiation of research by state agencies. In most cases the interest of state government personnel in particular research programs and their willingness to exercise initiative have existed independently of any expressed federal interest or its absence.[15]

Even on the subject of federal administrative controls there was some expression of approval from state scientific personnel. Penniman found in Wisconsin that the budget control maintained by the United States Labor Department Bureau of Employment Security "assures cooperative planning of employment security programs including the data gathering and analysis function."[16] In California state scientists were outspoken in their praise of the constructive way review and approval of research projects were handled in the area of fish and wildlife research. State officials reported no federal interference here and furthermore expressed the view that much of the state's research in this field would never have been undertaken without federal support.[17]

INTERSTATE RELATIONS IN SCIENTIFIC ACTIVITIES

The information in the six state studies on interstate relations in scientific research programs is fragmentary. Some collaborative activities were reported in the area of resource development, including small programs of research and some collection and analysis of data. Wisconsin, for example, reported participating in the Mississippi Flyway

operation of the nation's agricultural research program would indicate that the several experiment station directors, operating through the Association of Land Grant Colleges, have nearly decisive influence in the Office of Experiment Stations of the U.S. Department of Agriculture which is responsible for administering grants-in-aid to the states." *Ibid.*

15. Lehmann, Connecticut Report, Ch. 10.
16. Penniman, Wisconsin Report, Ch. 5.
17. Marshall, California Report, Ch. 4.

Council and gathering information on water pollution in cooperation with a number of neighboring states.[18]   Connecticut for its part functioned as a member of three interstate bodies, all of which have stimulated some small research undertakings in the resources area.[19]   California has been an active partner in the Pacific Marine Fisheries Commission, an interstate compact dedicated in part to coordinating marine fisheries research along the Pacific coast.   Studies sponsored by the Commission are conducted by state agency scientists in the member states.[20]   Some research undertaken by state fish and game organizations within the framework of the United States Fish and Wildlife Service programs also takes on the character of cooperative, interstate research.

In another area of governmental activity is the Crash Injury Project carried on by Cornell University Medical College.   It is financed by Department of Defense funds and uses data supplied by state motor vehicle departments. Four states (only North Carolina among the six under study here) are participating through collection of detailed information on automobile accidents.   In the area of agriculture, most experiment stations in the six states are more or less continually engaged in regional projects sponsored, organized, and financed by the United States Department of Agriculture through the Office of Experiment Stations.[21]

The above items represent all that was reported in the six state studies on the important scientific programs that were consciously planned and carried forward as cooperative activities of two or more states.   These bits of evidence hardly provide enough data to reach any conclusion about interstate relations in scientific activities.   In the study particular attention was focused on the various interstate com-

18. Penniman, Wisconsin Report, Ch. 4.
19. Lehmann, Connecticut Report, Ch. 10.
20. Marshall, California Report, Ch. 4.
21. These projects are instances of interstate cooperative research in the sense that representatives of the participating experiment stations plan the projects jointly, maintain contact during the conduct of the research, and review the results.

pacts these six states participate in, but this part of the investigation produced very little information about scientific activity.[22] Furthermore, no claim can be made to complete coverage of the many and varied interstate associations and organizations in which these states participate. For example, the state reports do not examine the role of the Council of State Governments or explore in detail the activities of the National Highway Research Board.[23] Again these studies have not gathered information systematically on the part played by the many associations of state officials.

While the data gathered on interstate relationships in scientific activity are thus too fragmentary and incomplete to provide the basis for firm generalization, one or two relevant comments can be offered. In the case of the interstate compact agencies it appears that for the most part they are little concerned with research or other scientific activities. Yet even from the brief examination attempted in this study it is quite evident that these interstate agencies perform a most useful communication function. In a number of cases they provide an opportunity for representatives of several states sharing certain common problems to meet together regularly for consideration of these problems and their solution. Although such agencies rarely sponsor, finance, or carry on scientific activity, it is undoubtedly true that the discussions held among state officials often generate ideas leading directly to scientific work undertaken by one or more of the participating states.

22. Even the Port of New York Authority carried on only a very small program of scientific activity in 1954. The scientific work was performed by Authority staff members or by private research organizations under contract. These scientific programs are not considered an extension of the scientific activities of the states that are members of the compact on which the Authority is based. Birkhead and Ahlberg, New York Report, Appendix, "The Port of New York Authority."

23. The Highway Research Board in performing its clearinghouse function may be providing the kind of connecting link or catalytic agent to make important parts of the state highway research programs take on the character of cooperative scientific activity among several states.

VI

The Scientist and the State

In this age of advanced technology state governments can carry on scientific programs adequate to the tasks before them only by staffing these programs with qualified research personnel. Once having recruited qualified personnel, state agencies must then provide the kind of environment that will enable them to perform their scientific work most effectively. Accordingly, this study of scientific activities in six states has tried to assess in a general way the work environment the state governments provide for scientific personnel. The material on this subject in the individual state studies is largely qualitative and varies in detail from program to program and state to state.

The study staff conducted interviews with a considerable number of professional personnel who were engaged in scientific activities. The interviews produced a variety of factors important in evaluating the work environment. As might have been expected, many of the same points were raised in all of the states and in nearly all of the agencies covered.

The factors descriptive of what research staff members want in their work situation can be conveniently grouped into three categories. The first category includes the personal considerations of salary, promotional opportunity, and job security. The second category, character of the organization, embraces a host of items related to the agency setting, such as: recognition of the importance and value of scientific work, relative independence from operating responsibility, freedom in the choice of subjects for study, stability of financial support and management policies, and adequacy of supporting facilities (laboratories, equipment, clerical and statistical assistance). The third category, professional opportunity, is composed of the following: publication opportunity, availability of additional training, opportunity to attend professional meetings and consult with qualified experts, and opportunity to associate as a co-worker with high-ranking scientists. The following discussion attempts a general description of the strengths and weaknesses of the states as employers of scientific personnel, employing the above criteria, which were supplied by the scientists themselves, as the basis for evaluation.

PERSONAL CONSIDERATIONS

Only New York and California among the six states have established salary scales enabling them to compete favorably for scientific personnel. Salary levels for research positions in both these states are comparable to those of federal agencies and major colleges and universities in the country; they are still well below income levels available in industry and in private professional practice. Particularly in the case of psychiatrists, other medical scientists, and engineers, even New York and California have experienced difficulty finding qualified people willing to accept research salaries.[1]

Connecticut, New Mexico, North Carolina, and Wisconsin all suffer from inadequate salary levels in their efforts to compete for research staffs. In Connecticut, for example, an agency head observed that one research project for which the legislature appropriated funds never materialized be-

---

1. Marshall states at one point: "Staff members in Mental Hygiene feel that California's salary schedule for medical personnel is the highest in the nation, including the United States Veterans Administration. Salaries, of course, are still far short of what a psychiatrist can earn in private practice." California Report, Ch. 6.

cause the state found it impossible to recruit the necessary staff at the established salaries.[2]

Promotional opportunities appear to be better in California than in the other states. The state budget has been rising steadily for a number of years, keeping pace with population growth and the increasing wealth and productivity of California's economy. In this situation research personnel can look forward to steadily expanding programs and good opportunity for professional advancement.[3] The New York Report, however, notes that state agency scientists complained particularly about "the relatively slow promotion of junior staff, and the difficulties involved in adjusting their pay to meet outside conditions."[4] Wisconsin's research personnel offered a similar criticism to the effect that promotions and salary increases "tend to occur only once a year at most."[5] In general, then, and aside from California, the state reports find some dissatisfaction about the slow pace of promotion and limited opportunity for professional advancement.

Throughout the six states research personnel in the agricultural experiment stations appear to enjoy the highest salary levels and the best research career opportunities of scientists in any state government agency. In California, for example, experiment station salaries are generally higher than those paid researchers in the United States Department of Agriculture. Furthermore, scientists can reach these top salary levels in an experiment station and still stay in research.[6] Yet despite these high salaries and good career opportunities there appears to be a real shortage of trained agricultural research personnel. At the same time that experiment stations are expanding their research programs, the

2. Lehmann, Connecticut Report, Ch. 9.
3. Marshall, California Report, Ch. 9.
4. Birkhead and Ahlberg, New York Report, Ch. 10.
5. Penniman, Wisconsin Report, Ch. 9.
6. Marshall, California Report, Ch. 9.

supply of research-minded graduate students in the colleges of agriculture is declining.[7]

Turning next to the question of job security, how far do merit systems in the six states cover professional positions in agencies carrying on scientific programs? As noted in Chapter I, four of these states have developed state-wide civil service systems, based on merit, which covered virtually all the agencies engaged in scientific activities in 1954. The remaining two states (New Mexico and North Carolina) apply the merit system only to those agencies in the health-welfare area where the United States Department of Health, Education, and Welfare requires one in accordance with federal standards as a condition to the receipt of certain grants. Research scientists in any of the states holding positions covered by merit systems are protected against arbitrary action by their agency head or other administrative superior.[8] In general, new entrants are recruited on the basis of competitive examinations designed to establish qualifications, and vacancies at higher levels are filled at least in part by promotional examination conducted among those eligible for the position.

Although state personnel systems thus provide some measure of job security, they also impose certain handicaps in the form of inflexible procedures and policies not geared to the needs of the competitive market for scientific personnel. For example, in Wisconsin the Conservation Commission reported particular difficulty in filling certain positions because the merit system made no provision for a higher starting salary for the applicant who had more than a bache-

7. Lehmann, Connecticut Report, Ch. 3.

8. It would be a mistake, however, to assume that the state government scientist has been accorded iron-clad security. For example, the scientist would have no recourse if the legislature should decide to abolish his position by the simple expedient of failing to appropriate any funds to his agency. Perhaps the uninspiring conclusion expressed by Connecticut's scientific personnel is the most precise statement that can be made, namely, that "there was no more insecurity in working for the state than in employment with educational institutions, private industry, or the federal government." *Ibid.*, Ch. 9.

lor's degree.[9]   In another situation, California's Division of Labor Statistics and Research expressed real concern over the problem of inbreeding, created largely by the refusal of the state Personnel Board to agree to recruitment from the outside to fill vacancies at the middle level. Indeed, Marshall reports: "Recently, the Division lost an opportunity to obtain an outstanding federal employee who was interested in and qualified to join the Division but was barred because the Personnel Board insisted on a promotional examination."[10] These difficulties are direct consequences of a civil service system and illustrate that the advantages of security are frequently purchased at some loss in flexibility.

CHARACTER OF THE ORGANIZATION

The most significant characteristic of scientific organizations that is attractive to research scientists is the sense of high value they accord to scientific inquiry. The scientific program agencies (those in which research is the central objective) are most likely to develop this kind of atmosphere. California and New York have tended more than the other four states to organize their research activities in such agencies or in units wholly devoted to scientific work. This fact is in itself evidence that the governments of these two states have accorded a special professional status to research scientists in recognition of the value of their contribution.[11]

In Connecticut, New Mexico, North Carolina, and Wisconsin the emphasis in scientific programs is placed much more directly upon operations and the achievement of operating

9. Penniman, Wisconsin Report, Ch. 4.
10. Marshall, California Report, Ch. 5.
11. Birkhead and Ahlberg comment on one disturbing note in the attitude of New York state officials towards employment of scientists: "The solution to this problem [the shortage of engineers] tended to be viewed as limited to meeting pay competition. Broader concern with the problems of attracting and retaining the young scientists and engineers was not evident. A fatalistic attitude prevails which reflects, in part, a widely accepted public belief that government employment must of necessity be second rate." New York Report, Ch. 10.

results than on research.   This emphasis inevitably lowers the status of the research scientist within the organization and subtly narrows the opportunity open to him to attain his professional objectives.   The situation reported by Lehmann in Connecticut's health, education, and welfare agencies is a typical illustration:

> Research project supervisors and staff in this functional area, especially those working within operational units and to a lesser extent those in separate organizations, indicated that lack of time to devote to research resulting from the pressures of routine tasks was the prime factor prohibiting more extensive research programs. Those working in separate research units felt that too much of their time had to be devoted to solving lesser operational problems that should not have been brought to the research organization.[12]

This situation in Connecticut, coupled with salaries too low to be competitive and limited promotional opportunities, can hardly fail both to discourage and to limit the effectiveness of the well trained research scientist.   Such an environment is not likely to attract men who are primarily research scientists[13] but rather individuals who, originally attracted to the agency by an interest in its substantive program, have some skills in trouble-shooting and assume the research tasks merely as a part of their operating responsibilities.[14] There is no intention here to be critical of such an arrangement; for many purposes it undoubtedly serves admirably. Where the role of research is conceived in this way, however, the work environment is probably not very attractive to the dedicated scientist.

12. Lehmann, Connecticut Report, Ch. 6.
13. It is true, of course, that in some situations the opportunity for professional research personnel to deal directly with operating problems proves a strong attraction.   Marshall notes that proximity to the "firing line" can challenge the interest of research scientists who are accustomed to devoting their energies to "broad surveys, fact finding and the development of policy."   California Report, Ch. 9.
14. Penniman, Wisconsin Report, Ch. 9.

All six states have some agencies with the characteristics of scientific program organizations. The agricultural experiment stations, New Mexico's Institute of Mining and Technology, Connecticut's Geological and Natural History Survey, and others help make the setting in their state governments generally more favorable for conducting scientific research and development. The special place of the University of Wisconsin as a research arm of state government strengthens the state's attraction to research scientists,[15] despite the fact that Wisconsin's regular agencies for the most part are oriented towards operations.

A second organizational characteristic important to the scientist is freedom in determining the subject of his research. In one sense this factor is a reflection of the value an agency places upon scientific inquiry. In another sense it is a by-product of organizational arrangements, for considerable freedom of choice tends to be associated with research programs composed of separately organized projects. The scientific program agencies for the most part use this project system. Typically, these agencies formulate general program emphases in advance, indicating broad priorities for groups of problems to be studied. Within this framework the individual researcher enjoys considerable latitude in selecting the subject for study and developing the initial outlines of the project.[16] These organizations are usually staff-oriented as distinguished from operations-oriented. Their underlying philosophy holds that the scientific contribution of the staff will be maximized by affording creative minds as much freedom as possible to pursue lines of inquiry in which their greatest interests lie. As noted earlier, California and New

15. *Ibid.*, Ch. 8 has a discussion of the close association of state agency officials and university research scientists.

16. Marshall, California Report, Ch. 3, and Richards and Radosevich, New Mexico Report, Ch. 4, contain descriptions of the research planning process in two agricultural experiment stations typical of scientific program agencies.

York allocate a larger share of their dollar and manpower resources available for scientific activities to organizations that embody this philosophy in their research programs. In all six states the agricultural experiment stations and state universities, as well as scientific program agencies such as the New Mexico Institute of Mining and Technology, rank high in terms of the freedom afforded research scientists in the selection and design of their research.

The third constructive organizational characteristic is the support given to scientific work in the form of stable or rising budgets, stable policies and direction from higher administrative levels, and adequate service facilities. The continued stability of financial support for research appears most likely in California, although certainly in the areas of health and mental hygiene New York has achieved a position of national pre-eminence in the support of research.[17] The wide differences in expenditures reported for the four areas of governmental activity in each of the states make generalization in this matter of support for scientific activity extremely difficult. In many ways the comparison of this distribution of expenditures from state to state is the best indicator available from this survey. Clearly the field of agricultural research was in high favor in terms of budgetary support in all six of these states, and probably the same was true in the other forty-two. Legislators appear willing to appropriate more and more funds to the agricultural experiment stations, responding to the well organized farm interests among their constituents. The experimental farms and excellent laboratories available to experiment station scientists also appear to set them apart from other less well supported groups of state agency scientists.

17. New York state's ability to attract and retain outstanding research scientists in its medical and mental health research programs offers support for this observation. Birkhead and Ahlberg, New York Report, Ch. 7.

PROFESSIONAL OPPORTUNITY

The final group of factors to be applied to the six states in an effort to understand their nature as employers of scientific personnel has to do with the opportunities provided for professional growth. Again most of these factors are more likely to be found in a government agency fitting the description of the scientific program organization. Accordingly, they are present to a greater degree in California and New York than in the other four states.

One important element in professional advancement of the research scientist is an opportunity to publish the results of his work for technical audiences. Such opportunity is likely to depend in part upon encouragement from superiors to prepare research material for articles and for papers to be read at professional meetings. Some agencies arrange for scientists to devote time to professional writing and provide clerical, statistical, and stenographic services to assist them. As noted earlier, some state agencies publish technical journals carrying articles prepared by staff members. Generally in all six states organizations such as the agricultural experiment stations, the fish and game research units, the water resource investigation agencies, and the minerals and geological research organizations encourage and often insist upon publishing the results of staff research and data collection.

Making technical training available to research personnel is another means of encouraging career development. The emphasis placed upon training programs usually is greatest in the health and public welfare fields, as was noted in the discussion of scientific activity expenditures in Chapter II.[18]

18. The data reported in this study on training of scientific manpower probably do not reflect accurately the efforts of various state agencies engaged in scientific activities to provide additional technical training for their research staff members. On-the-job training programs were not reported and in-service training activities qualified only where organized separately from on-the-job training. Accordingly, it is quite possible that state agencies in these states devoted much more attention to staff development through training in research skills than the expenditure figures suggest.

A third and most important aspect of professional growth lies in the opportunities afforded research scientists to associate, consult, and work with other scientists. These professional contacts may occur in a number of ways; two are of concern here: (1) attendance at meetings of professional societies, and (2) personal association as co-workers with highly qualified scientists of wide reputation.

In encouraging their research personnel to attend professional society meetings, state agencies in all six states must operate within the framework of established policies governing out-of-state travel. In the normal process, decisions authorizing travel beyond the borders of the state are likely to be made by the executive budget staff or the governor. In reviewing applications for travel to professional meetings, budget staffs tend to apply fiscal management criteria rather than standards derived from research program needs and considerations of staff career development. New Mexico, for example, requires that all out-of-state travel be authorized by the governor. Between the efforts of newspaper reporters, the Taxpayers Association, and politicians seeking to win votes on economy drives, the state's travel policy has become exceedingly restrictive. Richards and Radosevich observe:

> The reputation of the policy and the unfavorable publicity given out-of-state travel, however, make agency heads exceedingly reluctant to request additional travel funds and to approve formally the requests of their staff members. Indeed, the persons engaged in scientific activity who were interviewed for this study almost universally expressed a great need for more frequent attendance at professional meetings.[19]

Complaints about inability to attend professional meetings were almost universal among staff members engaged in scientific activities throughout the six states. State travel policies tend to be narrowly interpreted, and funds for travel are most inadequate. Certain agencies have eased the short-

19. Richards and Radosevich, New Mexico Report, Ch. 4.

age of travel funds somewhat by using federal money for trips to professional meetings. Also, some agencies, although not able to provide funds, will encourage staff members to go to such meetings by granting them time with full pay for attendance. Scientists in the six states are more irritated over restrictive travel policies than over any other single factor. Since professional contacts are so important to the scientist, he cannot understand a policy that may require him to decline an invitation to deliver a paper at some professional meeting, especially when his presentation would enhance the prestige of the state and his agency, as well as his own reputation.[20]

The second consideration regarding professional associations concerns the quality of an agency's scientific staff and the opportunity to work in a top-flight program as a member of a first-rate team of research scientists. Agencies in each of the six states afford such an opportunity to their younger scientists in varying degrees.[21] For example, New York's Psychiatric Institute with its nationally recognized staff furnishes less experienced researchers an almost unparalleled opportunity to associate with outstanding research scientists in the study of mental health. Sometimes the prestige of the staff is decisive in the recruitment of promising scientists.

State-federal programs of cooperative research and data gathering present another means for the state government scientist to expand his professional relationships at the working level. The Joint Federal-State Crop and Livestock Reporting Service is a case in point; it affords agricultural

20. Penniman, Wisconsin Report, Ch. 3; Marshall, California Report, Ch. 9; and Lehmann, Connecticut Report, Ch. 9.

21. Lehmann, in describing the Connecticut scientific personnel situation, observes: "Training and background of research personnel indicated a high level of professionalization, and nearly all research projects were conducted by Ph.D.'s or Ph.D. candidates. Indeed, association with competent and stimulating co-workers was commonly listed by research personnel as one of the main advantages of conducting research for state agencies." Connecticut Report, Ch. 9.

statisticians at both levels of government a broader experience than they would have if the program were confined to either the state or the federal government.[22]

Still another opportunity for professional development of state scientific personnel lies in the activities of various professional groups of state officials and of such organizations as the Council of State Governments. The evidence presented in the individual state studies on participation in the work of these associations is too uneven to attempt any general comparisons. The Wisconsin report, however, makes clear that the associations and the experience afforded through such organizations can be an important part of individual professional growth.[23]

A CONCLUDING NOTE ON PROFESSIONALISM

The individual state reports illustrate clearly the efforts of state scientific personnel to attain a high professional standard, in part stimulated by the cooperative federal-state programs. Marshall's description is characteristic of what was observed in every one of the six states:

> Scientists and operating officials come to know each other very well, and often identify themselves more closely with their common professions than with their respective levels of government. Generally speaking they regard themselves as foresters, geologists, or public health experts first, and employees of the state government or the federal government second. This being the case, and in the light of their many contacts fostered by grants-in-aid and an inevitable overlapping of jurisdiction, it is not surprising that state-employed scientists are heavily influenced by professional colleagues outside state government regarding the desirable scope, content, and methodology of state research undertakings.[24]

This development of a strong sense of professionalism and an attachment to a professional group and its standards is

22. Cleaveland and Johns, North Carolina Report, Ch. 3; and Penniman, Wisconsin Report, Ch. 3.

23. Penniman, Wisconsin Report, Ch. 4, Ch. 5, and Ch. 7.

24. Marshall, California Report, Ch. 9.

not unique with scientists at the state level. Indeed, Don K. Price calls attention to the part these professional bodies have played in developing the present significant role of science in the federal government.[25]

This growing professionalism can have important effects both upon the individual scientist and upon the agency conducting scientific work. First, in terms of the individual the emphasis upon the professional character of his work can be a strong stimulus to improved performance. Furthermore, the association with members of his professional group in other state agencies may perhaps convey to him some sense of a unified scientific effort within state government. Closer ties with its professional society may also affect an agency significantly. The professional group may serve as clearinghouse and coordinator for certain kinds of scientific work. Furthermore, by bringing scientists from different agencies and perhaps different states into closer communication and working relations, the professional society is at once promoting better coordination and laying the ground work for cooperation and collaboration in research.

Harvey Mansfield in his essay for The American Assembly conference on "The Forty-Eight States" raised an interesting question about the effect of this growing professionalism upon the governor's position as chief executive:

But cooperative federalism brings closer links between the professionals in subject matter agencies at the two levels—national and state health officials, highway engineers, and others. Each of these groups has its professional associations, its organized clienteles, its technical standards and goals. The effect of these vertical ties . . . is to promote specialization and insularity among state agencies, along with political demands for their autonomy in policy, for earmarked revenues, and so on. If these tendencies grow, what room is there for a governor trying to pull strings

25. Price, *Government and Science*, pp. 20-31.

together, to maintain a balance among his state's activities and to exercise some general managerial oversight?[26]

Mansfield's observations appear to fit the case of the researcher engaged in scientific activity. He identifies himself more with his professional group than with state government; he is not dependent for funds on the governor or the budget staff but on earmarked revenues and federal grants. Continued striving for professionalism and the autonomy associated with it would appear to be at cross purposes with the efforts towards more effective integration of state government under the leadership of a strong chief executive. If scientific research is to play an important role in policy making, then progress must be continued towards developing a real policy-making center in the institution of the governor. Yet, if scientific work is to attract the most promising young researchers, if it is to deal effectively with the most critical problems facing the states today, then it must be accorded high professional status in state government conducive to improved productivity, and scientists must be able to develop the *esprit de corps* and standards of performance that accompany a sense of professionalism. If Mansfield's analysis is correct, then these two objectives may pose a real dilemma.

26. Mansfield, "The States in the American System," *The Forty-Eight States*, p. 32.

VII

Summary and Conclusions

THE REPORTS on each of the six states present a wealth of specific information on research and development and related activities conducted by the agencies of these state governments. Describing these scientific programs and attempting some measurement of their scope in terms of dollars and manpower have been the first objectives of this study. Despite the great variety in detail from state to state recorded in this inventory, the analysis has revealed some evidence of pattern in the scientific programs of the six states. Earlier chapters in this monograph have attempted to highlight some of these patterns.

Expenditures for scientific activities in 1954 ranged from $2 million to $32 million in the six states. When considered as a percentage of total state expenditures for general governmental purposes, this investment in scientific work varied only between 1.25 and 2 per cent. Most of these funds were appropriated by the six state legislatures: from two-thirds to four-fifths of the scientific dollars in four states and about one-half in the remaining two. The federal government provided between one-fourth and one-third of the scientific dollars in five states and one-tenth of these funds in New York. Some 70 per cent or more of the expenditures for scientific activities in each of the states were allocated to the support of research and development. Of the remainder the largest part was invested in the collection of general-purpose data.

Distribution of scientific activity expenditures among the four major areas of governmental activity in the six states varied considerably, but within certain broad lines which suggest the faint outlines of a kind of pattern. In California, Connecticut, North Carolina, and Wisconsin, agriculture claimed a larger share of the dollars invested in scientific programs than any other area, from one-third to one-half. In the other two states agriculture ranked second, accounting for approximately one-fourth of scientific activity expenditures. In New York the area of health, education, and welfare ranked first, with 45 per cent of the scientific spending, while in New Mexico the field of resource development and public works came first with 42 per cent. Again in the first four states listed above, the state university area ranked second to agriculture and received between one-sixth and one-third of all scientific activity funds in 1954.

In regard to the character of research performed in these states in 1954 some suggestion of pattern also emerges. The relative emphasis placed upon basic research and applied research, as measured by the percentage of total research and development funds invested, shows another grouping of four states. In California, Connecticut, New York, and North Carolina approximately one-third to two-fifths of all funds available for research and development were expended on basic research. In the same states applied research claimed from one-half to two-thirds of the total funds invested in research and development. Wisconsin placed heavier emphasis upon basic research (approximately one-half) and correspondingly less on applied research (43 per cent); New Mexico deviated in the other direction, spending only one-fourth of its research dollars on basic research and investing almost three-fourths in applied studies. The state universities and the agricultural experiment stations carried on a very large portion of the research reported in every state except New York. In California, Connecticut, North Carolina, and

Wisconsin these two agencies expended from 92 to 100 per cent of the funds allocated to basic research and 75 per cent of these funds in New Mexico. The agricultural experiment stations alone accounted for from 40 per cent to 70 per cent of all expenditures for applied research in these five states. Only in New York did other agencies perform a significant role in the conduct of basic research. Life science research dominated the scientific activities in every one of the six states except New Mexico, where the emphasis upon resource development led to a heavier investment in physical science research than in life science studies. In the other five states, between one-half and three-fourths of the research dollars were expended on work in the life sciences. Expenditures for physical science research ranked second in four states, first in New Mexico and a poor third in New York. Studies in the social sciences accounted for less than 20 per cent in every state and reached a low of 8 per cent of total research and development expenditures in Wisconsin.

In 1954 the scientific activity program in the area of agriculture tended to be more fully developed than in any of the other three major areas of governmental activity. Expenditures ranged from $0.5 million to $10 million and represented from one-fourth to one-half of the total state scientific activity budgets. Without exception in these states the agricultural experiment stations accounted for the major scientific programs in agriculture. In the areas of resource development and public works and health, education, and welfare, by contrast, there were at least four to six state agencies carrying on important scientific programs. Research in the area of resource development and public works tended to be applied in character and the emphasis in terms of field of science varied widely. New York and Wisconsin emphasized life science studies in the areas of wildlife, fisheries, and forestry; California and New Mexico gave more attention to physical science research, while Connecticut and North Carolina emphasized social science studies built around economic development. Cooperative relationships in scientific work between state and federal government scientists proved to be especially rich in this broad area.

While expenditures for health, education, and welfare accounted for at least half of total state expenditures for general government in five of the six states (30 per cent in Wisconsin), only in New York did the investment in scientific activity in this area constitute a significant portion of total investment in scientific programs. New York in 1954 expended almost three times as much on scientific work in health, education, and welfare as the other five states combined. In California, Connecticut, and New York the health and mental health agencies received the large proportion of the scientific dollars available to health, education, and welfare agencies. In the remaining three states, by contrast, the public welfare and education agencies have tended to develop the more significant scientific activity programs as measured by dollar expenditures.

Three things characterize the state university as a separate area of governmental activity in scientific work: (1) in five states these institutions accounted for over half of all the basic research reported in 1954; (2) in four states these same state universities accounted for between 60 and 85 per cent of all the physical science research uncovered in the study; and (3) the state universities derived a larger proportion (at least 50 per cent in five states) of their annual research expenditures from the federal government than did agencies in any other area. Only in New York were state appropriations to the state university for research support in 1954 larger than the grants made by the federal government.

The study having identified, described, and to an extent measured this scientific effort in the six states, the remaining task has been to explore the role of science and scientific activity in the practice of state government. This objective has been much more difficult than the inventory phase. A major reason for the difficulty, and at the same time perhaps the major finding of the study, is the lack of awareness at top policy-making levels in these states of anything in the nature of a comprehensive state scientific effort. Whatever suggestion emerges from these pages of the concept of a state scientific program results largely from the study itself and the attempt made in the course of this research to achieve an over-view of the total scientific effort of each state during the year in question.

This absence of an official awareness of a government-wide scientific effort at the state level results in inadequate attention to the problem of balance. Yet if state governments are to maximize the value of their research and scientific activity programs, they must develop better facilities for comparing and examining expenditures for scientific programs in different areas of governmental activity. This development is essential to almost any systematic attempt to evaluate current scientific programs in an effort to strengthen and improve them. The authors of three of the state reports proposed that an approach to the solution of this problem lay in improving the facilities and procedures for central budget review. Specifically, they proposed that the scope of budgetary review of scientific programs be broadened to include such things as the following: a modification of budget and accounting systems to separate costs and estimates concerning scientific activities; the adoption of a performance, or program, budget system; the addition to central budget staffs of analysts, or a separate unit, specializing in review of budget requests for research; and introduction of the techniques of benefit-cost analysis into the budget process.[1] Such steps as these would make possible systematic examination of balance

---

1. Marshall, California Report, Ch. 9; Birkhead and Ahlberg, New York Report, Ch. 10; and Penniman, Wisconsin Report, Ch. 9.

in three important aspects of scientific activity: balance among different components of scientific activity (research, development, and related scientific work); balance among research expenditures in different areas of governmental activity; and balance in the allocation of state and federal funds to finance specific programs. In addition, the inauguration of these steps would lead to increased recognition of state scientific programs as a loosely unified body of activity.

Despite this finding in each of the six state reports that scientific activity has not generally gained recognition and acceptance as a separate, identifiable function of state government, there is clear evidence to support the general conclusion that scientific programs are contributing to the practice of state government in four different but interrelated ways. First, in a very real sense scientific activity at the state level is the handmaiden of government operations. Research, data collection, and related scientific work afford means through which the state can perform more effectively its normal service and regulatory functions. Thus scientists in the state department of agriculture identify particular insect varieties threatening crop damage and develop more adequate control measures. The highway engineers, experimenting with different combinations of speed zones and intersection designs, develop an improved system for bringing rural farm vehicular traffic through main arterial highways into an urban market.

Secondly, a number of important state agencies conduct scientific programs as a direct service to significant groups within the state. Thus the agricultural experts in the experiment station study the physiology of wilting in certain types of diseased plants important to the state's farm economy. The state's geologists survey particular rock formations seeking to locate certain sands in commercial quantity for the construction industry.

In the third instance, when the state faces a serious

problem requiring major governmental action, its governmental leadership, the governor, state legislators, and heads of major departments may turn to qualified researchers seeking factual data, trend analysis, and the informed judgment of trained scientists. Partly on the basis of the aid the research staff can give, they develop new policy, inaugurate new programs, modify or terminate existing laws and programs. Thus analysts on the staff of a joint interim committee of the state legislature collect, study, and analyze the experience of cities throughout the country in relying upon annexation efforts to solve the problems created by their outlying urban fringe areas. Economists in a state department of economic development survey the declining economy of a coastal area of the state, attempting to determine the potential effect on this economy of developing certain inland waterway and port facilities in the region.

Finally, research and data collection also serve state government as a tool for program planning and evaluation. Thus statisticians in a state department of public welfare continually analyze social and economic characteristics of selected groups receiving old-age assistance in order to evaluate present case loads and project the effect on current staffing patterns of proposed changes in eligibility for assistance. Or, officials of the state department of education survey the turnover, loss, and mobility of public school teachers in part to measure the effectiveness of current measures to improve teacher working conditions.

The individual studies indicate clearly that these states have made principal use of research to support and improve operating programs and as a governmental service to important groups in the state. These are for the most part intensely practical activities seeking to resolve today's operating problems or to satisfy the present needs of farmers or sports fishermen or some other articulate group in the state. Such scientific work will undoubtedly continue and, on the strength of its major contributions in these six states, it deserves to continue and to be expanded where a demonstrated need exists.

On the whole these six states have placed limited emphasis upon research as a means to aid policy making either through basic knowledge supplied by long-range studies or as an aid to program development. A number of the states, notably New York and California, have intermittently assigned scientific personnel to work on long-range studies to provide the basic knowledge for policy. These two states have used the temporary study commission and the interim legislative committee with particular effectiveness to lay the ground work for major policy decisions, often in the form of new legislation.[2] Again, to a lesser degree, all six states have made some use of research and data gathering as a staff service to evaluate existing programs and plan new undertakings.

Recalling Price's concept of the policy role that science and scientific research play at the national level, it is evident that these six state governments have tended to under-emphasize this policy-supporting dimension. There are many reasons apparent in the pages of the individual state reports to encourage giving concerted attention to more effective utilization of scientific resources as an aid and support for policy making. Such an objective calls for further emphasis on the development of staff scientific agencies and the establishment of research staffs to carry on long-range studies as required to serve policy makers. These developments would introduce better balance into the role of research and scientific activities in state government and strengthen the institutions of the state responsible for policy making.

2. Marshall, California Report, Ch. 7; and Birkhead and Ahlberg, New York Report, Ch. 8. Occasionally one of these six state governments has carried on scientific work to provide the basis for policy making by contracting with some private research organization to carry on the research. See, for example, Cleaveland and Johns, North Carolina Report, Ch. 4.

Index

Administration of scientific programs, organizations for, 101-7; program formulation of, 108-12; program coordination of, 112-16; disseminating the results of, 116-19. *See also* Scientific programs

Agencies, state. *See* State agencies

Agricultural experiment stations, expenditures for research in, 31, 32, 35, 37, 43, 45; manpower in, 46, 47; research in, 56, 59-61; personnel of, 134-35; mentioned, 26, 85, 87, 88n, 94, 96, 98, 102, 103, 108-9, 110, 114-15, 117, 124, 130, 138, 139, 140, 147, 148, 151. *See also individual state ones*

Agriculture, expenditures for scientific activities in, 24-26, 49-53, 54-59, 70n, 83-84; and federal support, 41, 43, 44; nature of scientific activities in, 53-54, 59-63; mentioned, 7-8, 17, 20, 21, 30, 64, 75, 86, 95, 99, 118, 129n, 130, 139, 147, 148. *See also* Departments of agriculture

Ahlberg, C. D., 4n, 12n, 36n, 53n, 59n, 60n, 63n, 72n, 82n, 84n, 99n, 101n, 104n, 105n, 107n, 109n, 111n, 114n, 117n, 119n, 123n, 125n, 126n, 127n, 128n, 131n, 134n, 136n, 139n, 150n, 153n

Aircraft industry, 7

Albany, N.Y., 30n

Alfred University, 30n, 36n

Anderson, W., 15n, 16n, 17-18, 19

Applied research, expenditures for, 32-33; in agriculture, 56-57; in resource development and public works, 65-66; in health, education, and welfare, 75-76; in state university, 88-89; mentioned, 22, 23, 28n, 96, 100, 103, 110, 147-48

Association of Land Grant Colleges, 129n

Atomic research, 24, 26

Basic research, expenditures for, 30-32; in agriculture, 56-57; in resource development and public works, 65-66; in health, education, and welfare, 75-86; in state university, 87-89; mentioned, 22, 23, 28n, 100, 101n, 103, 125, 147-48, 149

Birkhead, G. S., 4n, 12n, 36n, 53n, 59n, 60n, 63n, 72n, 82n, 84n, 99n, 101n, 104n, 105n, 107n, 109n, 111n, 114n, 117n, 119n, 123n, 125n, 126n, 127n, 128n, 131n, 134n, 136n, 139n, 150n, 153n

California, Department of Public Health, 37, 78, 111n, 125; Agricultural Experiment Station, 60, 61, 100n; Department of Agriculture, 62-63; Department of Public Works, 64; Highway Division, 64; Department of Mental Hygiene, 81, 112; Department of Natural Resources, 96n, 106; Division of Mines, 96n, 102; De-